Principles and Practices
of Christian Education

Principles and Practices of Christian Education

An Evangelical Perspective

Robert W. Pazmiño

Wipf and Stock Publishers
EUGENE, OREGON

Wipf and Stock Publishers
199 West 8th Avenue, Suite 3
Eugene, Oregon 97401

Principles and Practices of Christian Education
An Evangelical Perspective
By Pazmiño, Robert W.
©1992 Pazmiño, Robert W.
ISBN: 1-57910-950-0
Publication date: April, 2002
Previously published by Baker Book House, 1992.

To
women who have taught me about connections:
my mother, Laura Ruth Pazmiño
my wife, Wanda Ruth Pazmiño
my mother-in-law, Aida Melendez
my daughter, Rebekah Joy Pazmiño

Contents

Introduction

This work is a sequel to my earlier text, *Foundational Issues in Christian Education: An Introduction in Evangelical Perspective*, which discussed the biblical, theological, philosophical, historical, sociological, psychological, and curricular foundations of Christian education. A task named in that text, but not addressed in detail, was the formulation of principles and guidelines for the practice of Christian education. *Principles and Practices of Christian Education: An Evangelical Perspective* addresses that important task.

Christian education by its nature is a "preparadigmatic" discipline, in the sense that it lacks one dominant framework that guides all thought and practice.[1] Naming the preparadigmatic nature of Christian education celebrates the place of freedom and creativity in responding to the challenges of teaching and learning in the Christian faith. But working in a preparadigmatic discipline does not exempt Christian educators from the responsibility to develop principles and guidelines for practice that represent a model for or an approach to Christian educa-

---

1. Robert W. Pazmiño, *Foundational Issues in Christian Education: An Introduction in Evangelical Perspective* (Grand Rapids: Baker, 1988), 13–14.

tion.[2] In fact, each generation must formulate its approaches and models in being faithful to God's call to teach the gospel to current and future generations. Setting forth principles and practices for Christian education serves to outline the necessary forms to complement the freedom and creativity that each generation enjoys. In this work I will suggest a number of forms, principles, and guidelines for practice, but two underlying forms and two complementary principles are prominent in what follows.

The first form is the "educational trinity," which is integrated throughout the work. The educational trinity comprises three elements, content, persons, and context, that need to be balanced throughout the educational process. In fact, education in general can be defined as the process of sharing content with persons in the context of their community and society. Christian education will be further distinguished from education in general within the discussions that follow.

The second form is the five-task model of Christian education. The five tasks—proclamation, community, service, advocacy, and worship—are essential to the life and mission of the Christian church, and they serve to distinguish Christian education from general education. This model guides the planning, practice, and evaluation of Christian education.[3]

The first principle to guide the practice of evangelical Christian education is the principle of conversion. Conversion involves human reconnection with God, others, and the creation made possible by the grace of God; evangelical theology recognizes—in fact, insists on—the need for both personal and corporate transformation in life. The principle of conversion also implies a second, corresponding principle.

2. Robert A. Drovdahl raises questions about characterizing Christian education as preparadigmatic. See "Toward a Paradigmatic Christian Education," *Christian Education Journal* 11 (Spring 1991): 7–16. His pursuit of settledness and a paradigm may limit the place of freedom and creativity, but his pursuit of a framework for Christian education is to be affirmed. The pursuit of a framework and form is the focus of this work.

3. This model is also discussed in *Foundational Issues*, 40–46, as an integrated model that emerges from the study of the biblical foundations of Christian education.

That second principle, connection, serves as an integrating concept throughout this book. In relation to the educational trinity, this second principle connects the three elements of content, persons, and the context of community/society. In relation to the five-task model, this principle links the five tasks to each other in ten possible combinations. Connection is also implied in the exploration of various educational structures, which themselves form an interlocking web. The emphasis upon both principles, conversion and connection, addresses the fragmentation in the life and faith of the Christian community at the dawn of the twenty-first century.

These forms and complementary principles underlie the organization of chapters. Chapters 1 and 2 present principles from the recent past and those appropriate for challenges in the thought and practice of Christian education. They outline a model that uses the organizing principle of conversion derived from evangelical roots, but expands upon it to include both corporate and personal life. Chapter 3 describes the distinct educational structures that operate in modern industrial society and presents guidelines for the practice of education in some of these structures. The chapter also recognizes the dynamics operative in other structures. Chapters 4 and 5 look at the specific areas of educational content and methods, and respectively highlight the principle of connection and the model of Jesus as the master teacher. Each chapter provides guidelines for practice. The sixth and final chapter discusses basic considerations for the process of educational evaluation, making use of the underlying forms and principles emphasized throughout the work.

This work is offered as one perspective that I trust will encourage reflection, dialogue, and a serious effort by other Christian educators to name their principles and guidelines for the practice of education within and without the evangelical theological orbit. If it encourages reflection and discussion, then this work has accomplished its purpose. The work is intended to be an introductory textbook for courses at college and seminary levels, and it draws extensively upon secondary sources to encourage wider reading.

I am grateful to colleagues, especially Ronald Habermas, Eileen Starr, and Robert Drovdahl, who offered insightful suggestions that I incorporated in the text. I am also grateful to Deborah Perkins, who assisted in the preparation of the manuscript. Finally, I wish to thank the members of North American Professors of Christian Education who have supported and encouraged my work.

1

Principles from the Past

In the United States, the dominant culture values the present and the future but frequently ignores principles from the past that merit continuing emphasis. To remedy this situation, Christian educators can affirm educational principles embodied in the Christian faith and identified by educators in the recent past. These principles emerge from theological distinctives that evangelicals have named as they have sought to identify fundaments, or foundations, of orthodox Christian faith. Orthodoxy refers to right, true, and good beliefs that are consistent with the gospel of Jesus Christ and the apostolic tradition. By considering theology or orthodoxy, evangelical educators affirm the determinative role of theology for the thought and practice of Christian education. As Stanley Hauerwas observed, what we believe, think, and feel makes all the difference in what we do and who we are.[1]

The focus upon orthodoxy provides a point of entry for exploring the evangelical heritage and represents the general emphasis in Protestantism upon the teaching of true beliefs and theological doctrines. Such a focus does not negate the importance of orthopraxis (true living or practice) and

1. Stanley Hauerwas, *Character and the Christian Life: A Study in Theological Ethics* (San Antonio: Trinity University Press, 1975), 227–28, 125.

orthopathos (true passion or commitment).[2] Donald G. Bloesch, an evangelical theologian, identifies the common elements in evangelicalism while recognizing the diversity of its various streams: Evangelicals have in common a "commitment to the revelation in Scripture over human philosophy, a poignant awareness that we are saved only by divine grace, a belief in the necessity for personal faith for salvation, and fidelity to the great commission to convert the world to the gospel."[3] Bloesch sees as the strengths of evangelicalism its Christocentric emphasis (orthodoxy), its fostering of personal piety (orthopathos), and its concern for mission and evangelism (orthopraxis). He also identifies as its weaknesses tendencies toward individualism, biblicism, ghettoism, sectarianism, privatism, and obscurantism.[4] Recognizing the importance of both orthopraxis and orthopathos, Christian educators can explore basic principles that emerge from the affirmation of theological beliefs or concepts.

Basic Orthodox Principles

The Statement of Faith of the National Association of Evangelicals, adopted in 1943 by representatives of some fifty denominations, set forth seven theological concepts.[5] In relation to each of these concepts, evangelical educators identify educa-

2. The distinctions between orthodoxy, orthopraxis, and orthopathos are explored in chapter 5. See Samuel Solivan, "Orthopathos: Interlocutor between Orthodoxy and Praxis," *Andover Newton Review* 1 (Winter 1990):19–25.

3. Donald G. Bloesch, "Evangelicalism," in *Harper's Encyclopedia of Religious Education*, ed. Iris V. Cully and Kendig B. Cully (San Francisco: Harper and Row, 1990), 235. Also see Donald W. Dayton and Robert K. Johnston, *The Variety of American Evangelicalism* (Knoxville: University of Tennessee Press, 1991) and Robert W. Pazmiño, *Foundational Issues in Christian Education: An Introduction in Evangelical Perspective* (Grand Rapids: Baker, 1988), 49–60.

4. Bloesch, "Evangelicalism," 236. Individualism is "every person wanting to do his or her own thing"; biblicism is treatment of the Bible "apart from both church tradition and historical study"; ghettoism, "a Christ-against-culture stance"; sectarianism, "Christians are encouraged to withdraw from other churches"; privatism, "the spiritual mission of the church often eclipses its social or cultural mandate"; and obscurantism, "a literal interpretation of the Bible brings the faith into conflict with modern science."

5. *Constitution of the National Association of Evangelicals*, 1–2.

tional principles of continuing significance that build upon this theological foundation.

The Bible as the Inspired and Authoritative Word of God

The Bible provides the essential, though not exclusive or exhaustive, content of Christian education. Sharing biblical content includes careful consideration of a variety of other educational factors. A caricature promoted by Harold William Burgess in *An Invitation to Religious Education* attributes to evangelical educators a "traditional theological approach" that depends exclusively on transmissive methods of teaching; by implication these methods are unresponsive to age-appropriate concepts and experiences.[6] This caricature, although it has some basis in fact, does not give a complete picture.

An approach that focuses on the Bible, implied by an emphasis on biblical content, does not exclude valuable insights derived from the study of the multifaceted dimensions of God's creation. Scripture itself validates our study and appreciation of nature (Ps. 19). Paul cites the insights gained through reason and experience in his appeal to conscience and the creation (Rom. 1–2). The creation, God's creation, includes the complexities of people in their personal and corporate lives. An affirmation of biblical authority enables Christian educators to affirm God's truth wherever it is revealed in creation. Such an affirmation also provides a standard, a measure for discerning truth in areas of general revelation. Such a standard enables Christians to bring into question all insights relative to a Christian life and world view. A Christian life and world view, if it is to be identified as Christian, must be consistent with the revelation of Christ in the Scriptures. In addition, such a view enables Christians to develop a comprehensive understanding of education.

Both Jesus' and Paul's lives exemplified such an approach. Jesus suggests that Christians can and should learn from happenings in the world (Luke 16:8). Paul unashamedly cited pagan poets on Mars Hill when he addressed the Athenians. Through-

6. Harold William Burgess, *An Invitation to Religious Education* (Birmingham, Ala.: Religious Education Press, 1975), 21–58.

15

out church history, Christians have carefully used reason, experience, and tradition in addition to the Scripture to discern truth.

An approach that emphasizes the Scriptures does not exclude careful study and wrestling with the biblical text and context. It does not exclude the tasks of exegesis and hermeneutics, or the responsibility of contextualizing God's truth for contemporary cultures. But this approach does include an appropriate reverence for the sacred text as God's vehicle for disclosing God's person and God's intentions for creation. Christian educators are called upon to share responsibly, not transmit mechanically, God's Word. This sharing requires proclamation and dialogue that enable various age groups to understand God's truth, to grapple with the implications of God's truth for their lives, and to respond in reverence and obedience to discerned truth.[7]

Christian education in the evangelical tradition is distinct from other traditions in its relatively exclusive centering upon biblical authority and content as the guideline for faith and practice. Certainly evangelical Christians, like other Christians, struggle with their selectivity in dealing with the truths of Scripture and with traditions that are not questioned. They also struggle with personal and corporate blindness in dealing with sins, inconsistencies, and contradictions. Yet they have a stated intention to be faithful to the biblical witness and consciously struggle with accountability in terms of biblical revelation. In considering the letter of God's Word, Christian educators hope that the spirit of God's revelation can be discerned for a faithful life of Christian discipleship in the modern world. Given the human situation, the fruits of these efforts for faithful living are mixed. This is also the case for Christian communities with theological distinctives that cannot be identified as evangelical. The danger in any theological tradition is to take a stance of arrogance that rejects the possibility that new truth and light can be discerned from God's Word.

The Oneness of God

The one God affirmed by Christians is revealed in three persons, the Trinity. Christians have often asserted that their

7. Lawrence O. Richards discusses these areas in *Creative Bible Teaching* (Chicago: Moody, 1970), 51–63.

efforts in Christian education, as in all areas of life, need to be God-centered. The meaning of such an assertion requires careful consideration, for the orthodox may make assertions and perpetuate shibboleths that they do not affirm in life and practice. When this occurs a dead orthodoxy exists.

A God-centered approach to education can be distinguished from approaches that center upon different foci. Hollis L. Caswell, an educator and curriculum theorist in the 1930s, identified a framework that distinguishes three foci for education (see fig. 1). He described students' interests, social functions, and organized knowledge as elements that are central to different philosophical perspectives in education.[8] In a relative and comparative sense, educators have emphasized one of the three elements as having priority and therefore as being determinative for effective teaching and learning. But in emphasizing one of the three foci, educators generally argue, the other two foci are in some way also addressed.

Figure 1
The Foci of Education

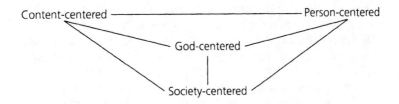

Educators who emphasize persons' or students' interests advocate a person-centered approach. This approach places priority upon assessing the students' felt needs, interests, and problems. These needs, interests, and problems guide the teacher and the students in the classroom and in activities outside the classroom. Such an approach values the individualization of

8. Hollis L. Caswell and Doak S. Campbell, *Curriculum Development* (New York: American Book Company, 1935), 141–89.

teaching and learning because of the diversity that exists among students. Psychological ordering of material is given priority over the logical ordering that typifies the content-centered approach. This is the case because of concern for the readiness of individuals to deal with content and sensitivity to "teachable moments" in the life of each student. A person-centered approach emphasizes discovery and self-directed inquiry as central to education, and it tends to see the teacher primarily as a facilitator of learning. Advocates of this approach contend that the content and context of education can be adequately considered only after one first focuses on the persons engaged as students and on "teachable moments" in their educational journeys.

"Teachable moments," a phrase that was popularized by Robert Havighurst, refers to occasions when students are highly motivated and prepared to learn new ideas, skills, or values.[9] In order to take advantage of these occasions or teachable moments, the teacher needs to focus upon individual students, questioning them and responding to cues indicating interest and need. Examples of such an approach in Christian education are the use of a survey of a youth group's interests to schedule weekly topics and the use of learning centers to encourage discovery learning and the pursuit of individual interests in a Sunday school children's class. As is the case with other approaches, a person-centered approach is subject to extremes. An extreme advocacy of this approach might ignore concerns for social responsibilities and organized knowledge. It might emphasize freedom to explore individual interests to the detriment of necessary structure, form, or discipline. Individuals need to be introduced to the accumulated wisdom of humankind and to their corporate and communal responsibilities beyond personal interests and needs.

Educators who emphasize social functions advocate a society- or community-centered approach. In contemporary discussions this approach emphasizes the need to contextualize. This approach places priority upon the anticipated needs of and expectations for students in relationship to responsibilities and

9. See Robert Havighurst, *Developmental Tasks and Education* (New York: David McKay, 1952).

roles in the community or society. Students are being prepared for their present or future roles as members of various groups. One example of this approach in Sunday school is training children to actively participate in worship. Children learn the books of the Bible in order to actively follow the reading of Scripture during the worship service and learn how to pray. Among the dangers inherent in an exclusive emphasis upon the society-centered approach is perpetuation of the status quo, even if current patterns of interaction may need to be changed, and a limitation of the creative response and inquiry that is characteristic of the person-centered approach. The society- or community-centered approach generally relies upon the processes of socialization and enculturation to enable students to acquire those values, attitudes, and understandings that facilitate participation in a given group. Unlike the psychological order for teaching and learning that characterizes the person-centered approach, this approach emphasizes the communal, cultural, or sociological order of the content. This order refers to the progressive acquisition of skills and competencies necessary to become an ideal participant in a particular community, contributing to and perpetuating its life.

The preceding description of a community- or society-centered approach emphasizes conformity and perpetuation of the status quo. But it is also possible to identify this approach with an effort to transform or revolutionize a society or to establish a community as an expression of ideals and values that are not embraced by the wider society. Thus education can play a reconstructionist role, providing an alternative to the status quo and a means by which to question prevailing norms for society. Such an alternative community might envision its mission as providing a protected and guarded space that may further the larger task of reform, renewal, or revitalization of society. For example, some Christians stress the need for Christian schools and home schools as an alternative to public schools that do not integrate their teachings with the Christian faith. Advocates of this approach contend that persons and content can be considered only in the light of the larger community and society that affect the educational experience.

19

The third approach described by Caswell is the subject-centered or content-centered approach. Educators who advocate this approach place priority upon organized knowledge and the structures inherent in the study of a particular field or discipline. The nature of the content guides the teaching and learning process; concern is for the logical order of the subject matter and adequate coverage of the material. The content-centered educator considers the demands of being initiated into a new field of study and provides students access to past and current contributors in that field. The potential weaknesses of an exclusively content-centered approach include failure to consider absorption and retention of the material by students and the relationships of the content to current and future life. An additional concern is the relationship of organized knowledge in one field or discipline to that of other fields and the transfer of learning from one field to another. A content-centered approach might not address such relationships as it also emphasizes intellectual inquiry. The acquisition of content may have no relationship with the life of persons and communities outside of the educational setting. This can readily be seen in curricula for a new believers' class that does not consider the age of participants or a varied approach to an agenda.

Educators who contend that the content or the subject is central argue that sharing and discovery of knowledge, understanding, and wisdom are key tasks. A concern for persons and the community and society may represent a preoccupation with the present and future that fails to recognize the heritage accumulated in various bodies of knowledge and available to persons and communities willing to engage in rigorous intellectual inquiry. To opt for another approach, they argue, is to sell the birthright of education for an unsatisfying porridge of personal or societal relevance.

These three approaches might be roughly compared with hosts' considerations in preparing a meal. One host, the content-centered advocate, is primarily concerned with the detailed preparation and serving of the food itself and in making the elements of the menu consistent. Another host, the society-centered advocate, is primarily concerned with the choice of the food in relation to the group assembled. This host also considers the nutritional content of the food in terms of preparing the guests for the activities during and following the meal, and furthermore thinks about the ambience or context for sharing the meal. The third host, the person-centered advocate, desires to please each guest and is sensitive to the individual tastes of those invited. From this analogy it is possible to note that the contribution of each host can be appreciated and can make for a successful meal. If we use the analogy of meal preparation, we can define teaching as an artfully prepared table welcoming participation.[10] Caswell, linking two metaphors, contends that like the host or the cook, the educator can act like a chemist to process the elements of students' interests, social functions, and organized knowledge in teaching effectively. To do so, discernment and wisdom are needed, and both qualities suggest that teaching is more of an art and a craft than a science. Caswell's metaphor of a chemical process might reduce teaching to an equation.

Using Caswell's framework, it is possible to conceive of combinations of emphases that involve the three centers. Indeed, various educators have advocated such combinations (see table 1).[11] It is also possible to conceive of the alternation of emphases within a particular class or group over time. Given the possible variations and combinations of emphases, the problem for the educator is how to maintain an adequate balance in one's class, curriculum, or educational program. Without all too conveniently calling upon God as the cosmic synthesizer at this point, Christian educators have proposed that a God-centered education offers an alternative and that a Christian world and life view provides distinctives to guide the entire educational process. What then is a God-centered approach to education, and how is it related to Caswell's framework?

A God-centered or combination approach establishes as its starting point the authority of God as revealed through Scripture, illumined by the Holy Spirit, and discerned through the operation of human reason and experience, both corporate and

10. This image for teaching is discussed in chapter 4.
11. Ronald G. Habermas developed this chart based upon the work of Caswell and Campbell, *Curriculum Development*, 141–89, and Pazmiño, *Foundational Issues*, 111–13.

21

Table 1
Educational Approaches

	Focus	Needs	Curriculum	Emphases	Limitations	Ministry Examples	Illustration (of Meal Preparation)
Student's Interests	Person-centered	"Felt" needs and interests of students	Psychological ordering (e.g., "What do you want to study?")	Teachable moments; "a-ha" experience	May ignore social responsibilities and/or organized knowledge	Youth group voluntary interest groups with discovery learning	Personal tastes and preferences ("What is John's favorite dessert?")
Social Functions	Community or society-centered	Anticipated needs and expectations of community	Cultural ordering (e.g., "What would benefit the group?")	Socialization (enculturation) processes	Tendency to perpetuate status quo; restricted inquiry and creativity	Junior church designed to train children for adult worship service	Food choices dependent upon corporate guests ("What nutritional guidelines should be used to meet the group needs of the two diabetic guests?")
Organized Knowledge	Content or subject-centered	Needs related to adequate coverage of material	Logical ordering (e.g., "What represents the best sequencing of the material?")	Prescribed value of universal subjects and curriculum?	Potentially ignore limits of cognitive, formal education; disintegration of material; transfer of learning neglected	Junior high youth learning denominational catechism	Coordination of menu to itself ("Which dessert would be most appropriate with this entree?")

individual. From the Scriptures, viewed as a trustworthy guide for Christian faith and practice, one can derive essential principles that influence educational thought and practice. One such guiding principle is the affirmation that all truth is God's truth, which implies a unity in truth and a correspondence between revealed truth and reality. This principle calls for the joyful acceptance of the truths in Scripture without subjection to a rigid literalism. The Christian is not exempt from the tasks of hermeneutics and the challenge to contextualize biblical truths in contemporary settings. But a God-centered approach does subject all truth claims to scriptural scrutiny while recognizing that the Bible is not an exhaustive source of truth and knowledge. Thus, any truth claims are initially judged in terms of their consistency with a Christian world and life view. A God-centered approach does not neglect knowledge discerned through nature, rationality, tradition, history, intuition, and even imagination. But insights derived from these sources are always subject to the light of biblical and theological reflection. This approach recognizes that certain educational issues are not resolved by flippant proof-texting or simplistic referral to biblical principles that ignores adequate grappling with the questions. For example, appeals to personal experience in many educational decisions must be subject to the biblical and theological scrutiny implied in a God-centered approach.

Some scholars may object to the use of the term *God-centered* to denote one approach. They suggest that the term alone is authoritative and therefore suggests arrogance. By use of this term I do not intend to identify this approach as final or beyond question, but rather to suggest the need for a holistic approach that embraces all of created life, which includes persons, communities, and subject matters. This term also implies that the center is indeed God and God's revelation in education and all of life. Another possible term for this approach is "educational trinity," which denotes the three essential educational elements of content, persons, and the context of community/society that are understood in relation to God's entire revelation. Nevertheless, the presence and operation of the educational trinity is an essential form for guiding the thought and practice of Christian education. It is an underlying form that is based upon the principle of affirming God as the center of life and therefore of education.

The educational trinity can be discussed in relation to a theological understanding of the Godhead as Trinity that is affirmed in the Christian faith.[12] God as Father/Creator can be seen as the source of all truth and content, with content being one element of the educational trinity. From the first person of the Trinity all knowledge and all wisdom originate, emanate, or issue, as was the case in the creation. God as Son/Redeemer, the second person of the Trinity, was incarnate in Jesus of Nazareth, the Christ. The Son appeared as a person, one who redeems and transforms humans through their faith in him. Christ's person and work therefore have a particular connection with the second element of the educational trinity, namely, person(s). God as Spirit/Sustainer can be seen as the formative agent in the birthing of the Christian community, the church, at Pentecost. The Holy Spirit continues the work of forming and activating the faith community, and as the spirit of life in the wider society brings about transformation and restrains the destroyers of life. Thus the third person of the Trinity can be connected with the third element of the educational trinity, the context of the community/society.

Three other insights also derive from the starting point of Christian theology and the Trinity.

The sovereignty of God and human responsibility. All human activity, including education, must be seen in terms of God's rule or reign over creation and God's design and purposes. The ultimate educational encounter is between God as the teacher and humanity as God's students or disciples. All persons involved in education are subject to God, are students of

12. The use of the term *trinity* in relation to educational foundations affirms the multiple-level understanding possible in this doctrine for all of life. The Trinity affirms a diversity of three along with a unity that brings wholeness and integration. See Max L. Stackhouse, *Public Theology and Political Economy* (Grand Rapids: Eerdmans, 1980), 32–34. Stackhouse suggests that a full appreciation of the theological trinity implies a tripartite analysis of various areas of human experience, which for the author includes education. A tripartite or trinitarian analysis proposes neither uniformity nor unending plurality, but unity amid a limited diversity, which is best modeled for us in the community of Creator, Redeemer, and Sustainer of the one true God.

God's truth, and are responsible to God for their lives. Christian education recognizes God as Sovereign and Creator and teachers and students alike as God's creation. Both teachers and students owe to God moral, ecological, religious, political, aesthetic, and intellectual responsibilities.[13] To complement the responsibilities, the promise given to Christians includes access to God's strength and the privileges of communion with God. Teachers have access to the very resources of God to meet the challenges of relating to students and communicating effectively. Students can look to the very resources of God to meet the challenges of study and training. With God as the teacher the challenge for teachers and students alike is to have a teachable spirit in approaching the tasks of education.[14]

The pre-eminence of God the Redeemer/Liberator and human response to Jesus Christ. A God-centered approach within the Christian community also recognizes that God has been revealed most explicitly in the person and work of Jesus of Nazareth. Primary questions for persons participating in Christian education efforts in this approach are: What have we done with Jesus Christ? Have we responded to him as our personal Lord, Savior, and Teacher? Have we exalted his name as Lord in our life and ministry personally and corporately? Have we shared the riches of his teachings? Are we responsible to his call in the world and sensitive to his agenda? Such questions pose a continuing challenge to teachers and students, a challenge implied in being a disciple of Jesus. This Christocentric approach recognizes it is Christ "in whom are hidden all the treasures of wisdom and knowledge" (Col. 2:3); thus all teaching and learning must be questioned in relation to his teachings, and the tasks of Christian education evaluated in terms of teaching others to obey all that Jesus commanded (Matt. 28:20). Jesus' teaching ministry serves as a model for Christian educators.

The indispensability of God the Spirit and human dependence upon the Spirit. A Christian approach maintains a super-

13. See Nicholas P. Wolterstorff, *Educating for Responsible Action* (Grand Rapids: Eerdmans, 1980), 33ff., for a discussion of these responsibilities.
14. See Richard R. Osmer, *A Teachable Spirit: Recovering the Teaching Office in the Church* (Louisville: Westminster/John Knox, 1990).

natural world and life view that points to the crucial role of the Holy Spirit in the task of education. The role of the Holy Spirit in teaching has been discussed by Christian educators such as Roy B. Zuck and Lois E. LeBar.[15] Christian educators are called to be responsive to the teaching of the Holy Spirit and to recognize that the Spirit guides persons "into all truth" (John 16:13).

All three principles point to the necessity and the wonder of divine and human cooperation in the tasks of education. Without the role of God the Creator, Redeemer, and Sustainer, Christian education can claim no dynamic distinctive from other educational approaches founded upon other world and life views. Christian educators do not assume a monopoly upon God's activities in education, but assume the need for a conscious dependence upon God and an interdependence with God so that education can change people's lives.

Another distinctive of a Christian approach is its ending point, namely, the glory of God. As the Westminster Confession states, the chief end of persons is to glorify and enjoy God forever. The chief end of all educational efforts of Christian persons, therefore, is to glorify God. How one glorifies God requires consideration and constant evaluation in relation to God's will and purposes. God is glorified to the extent that persons love God with all their heart, soul, mind, and strength, and love their neighbors as themselves. This love also evidences one's obedience to Christ as Lord, who commanded his disciples to love one another as Jesus himself loved them.

A Christian approach, as distinguished by its starting and ending points, affirms the insights offered by those who advocate person-centered, society-centered, and content-centered approaches. It is important to teach content to persons in the context of their community and society. But it is more important to help students discover a Christian perspective on various subjects, on themselves and others, and on their community and society. First, a Christian world and life view affirms the multifaceted aspects of truth as discerned through various dis-

15. See Lois E. LeBar, *Education That Is Christian* (Old Tappan, N.J.: Revell, 1981), and Roy B. Zuck, *Spiritual Power in Your Teaching*, rev. ed. (Chicago: Moody, 1972).

ciplines and subjects. It affirms intellectual pursuits within the context of loving obedience to God. Second, a Christian world and life view recognizes the infinite worth and dignity of all persons because they are created in the image of God. Third, this view attests to the appropriate concern for human responsibilities in relationship to human communities. With regard to how persons adequately address the concerns and values as represented by each of Caswell's centers, a God-centered approach appeals to various principles. One such principle has been clearly stated in Jesus' teaching in the Sermon on the Mount. It is summarized in Matthew 6:33: "But seek first God's reign and righteousness, and all these things will be given you as well." Devotion to God's reign sets in proper perspective all the treasures of wisdom and knowledge, all the unique needs and interests of individuals, and all the dynamics of communities and societies. Caswell's model is better described as an educational trinity affirming the place of persons, content, and the context of community/society.

The Deity and Humanity of Jesus Christ

The distinctive focus of the Christian faith is the person and work of Jesus Christ. Jesus Christ is proclaimed to be the revelation of God, the visible expression of the invisible God, and the unique Son of God. In his earthly ministry he made remarkable claims to be the way, the truth, and the life (John. 14:6). Thus the only acceptable nexus or point of integration for Christian education is Jesus Christ.

Jesus Christ functions as the point of integration in six areas of one's educational approach: goals, content, teachers, students, environment, and evaluation.[16]

Goals. The basic goal of Christian education is to enable persons to become obedient disciples of Jesus Christ. This is the educational mandate given the followers of Jesus Christ (Matt. 28:18–20). Initially, this mandate includes calling persons to belief and trust in Christ. Subsequently, it includes a life of discipleship. Marianne Sawicki describes the nature of Christian discipleship in terms of four elements: a personal encounter

16. Burgess suggests these basic categories in *An Invitation to Religious Education*, 12–13, in discussing different approaches in religious education.

27

with Jesus, a call to which one responds, a mission to testify to others about Jesus, and a following of Jesus to death.[17] Throughout the New Testament Jesus Christ is presented predominantly as Lord. The challenge posed for Christians is to affirm Christ's lordship in all areas of personal and corporate life. In the struggle to accept and conform to the implications of Christ's lordship, Christians are assured that in him are hid all the treasures of wisdom and knowledge (Col. 2:2–3).

Content. The central content of Christian education is the teachings of Jesus and the Christian tradition, described broadly to include the writings of the New Testament along with the Old Testament. LeBar describes this content as the living Word of God (Christ) and the written Word of God (the Bible).[18] To this formula must be added the revelation of God in nature. Additional content from the sources of reason, experience, and imagination must be considered, but all are subject to the framework and values of Christian truth. Christ is considered to be the theme, the underlying principle, and the heart of the content.[19]

Teachers. Christian educators often affirm that Jesus Christ is the ideal teacher, the teacher of teachers, and that his model is a constant challenge for both Christians and non-Christians. (One can question this affirmation because, in the light of his earthly ministry, his efforts can be evaluated as unsuccessful. This question will be explored in chapter 5, but it is assumed valid for discussion here.) Jesus completely incarnated the truths of his message in his teachings and life. He exemplified a remarkable sensitivity to the needs of his students and thereby tailored his content and methods to those needs. Even as they recognize the divine character of Jesus' insights and abilities as a teacher, and the unique redemptive nature of Jesus' teaching ministry, contemporary Christian teachers can still gain much through a careful study of Jesus' teaching.

It is essential that Christian teachers be, in fact, Christian. A Christian has a personal faith in and an identity with Jesus

17. Marianne Sawicki, *The Gospel in History: Portrait of a Teaching Church, The Origins of Christian Education* (New York: Paulist, 1988), 60, 62, 90.

18. LeBar, *Education That Is Christian,* 212–15.

19. Burgess, *An Invitation to Religious Education,* 38.

Christ and seeks to follow Jesus as the Christ. It is difficult to imagine a teacher nurturing others in a faith that is not alive and personally appropriated in his or her life. Teachers are also called to be students of Christ in order to effectively represent him in the classroom.

Students. Students in Christian education are called, along with their teachers, to an increasing conformity to the person and will of Jesus Christ. Students are created in the image of God and are therefore individually worthy of respect and dignity in and out of the classroom. Students along with teachers are responsible to Christ for their lives in the educational encounter and beyond.

Environment. Christian educators are sensitive to various dimensions of the environment, and D. Campbell Wyckoff has identified three such dimensions: the natural, the human, and the divine or the supernatural.[20] The centrality of Christ can be related to each of these three dimensions. The apparent connection is to relate the work of the Spirit of Christ and the exalted reign of Christ to the divine or the supernatural dimension of the environment. The challenge in Christian education is to create environmental conditions whereby the Spirit of Christ may work effectively in the lives of persons in the classroom, community, home, or church. In the human dimension of the environment, Christ has modeled commitments, interactions, and concerns among persons that can guide teachers, students, parents, and other persons. An equal concern for truth and love was incarnated in Jesus' relationships with others. In relation to the natural dimension of the environment, Jesus in his teaching demonstrated flexibility in the use of material resources and sensitivity to the consideration of such factors as visibility, mobility, student comfort, and stimulus variation.

Evaluation. The ultimate standard for evaluation of Christian education is whether the efforts bring glory and honor to the name of Jesus Christ. Are persons well prepared for lives of service in various areas of endeavor and ministry? Is the body of Christ edified and encouraged to mature in the faith and knowledge of Jesus Christ? Are the causes of his reign advanced in

20. D. Campbell Wyckoff, *The Task of Christian Education* (Philadelphia: Westminster, 1955), 104.

the world? This evaluation calls teachers, students, and others involved to consider the values of Jesus' reign in their teaching and learning. Chapter 6 will discuss evaluation in relation to Christian values.

The Salvation of Lost and Sinful Persons

George R. Knight has identified the effects of sin as they affect a Christian view of education:

> The essence of Christianity and Christian ethics is death—crucifixion—of self, pride, self-centeredness, and self-suffi-ciency, and a new birth in which we act upon a different set of principles because of our new relationship to Jesus Christ (Rom. 6:1–6; Matt. 16:24; Gal. 2:20; John 3:3, 5) . . . What is needed is transformation (metamorphosis) of our minds, cru-cifixion of our selves, and a spiritual rebirth so that we become new creatures with God and God's attributes at the center of our existence (Rom. 12:2; Phil. 2:5–8; 2 Cor. 5:17). Paul noted that this renewal is a daily experience, and Jesus remarked that the transformation was accomplished through the power of the Holy Spirit (1 Cor. 15:31; John 3:5).[21]

Christian educators recognize that sin has affected all dimensions of personal life, including intellectual life. A question posed for Christian educators is, Can truth be apprehended directly by fallible human beings? Christians can respond that this apprehension is possible only by the grace of God through general and special revelation and by the illumination of the Holy Spirit.

Christians have not, however, readily identified and addressed the effects of sin upon all dimensions of communal and societal life. In the nineteenth century evangelicals addressed communal and societal evils through fervent ministries, but these concerns faded during the fundamentalist/modernist tensions of the early twentieth century.[22] In the twentieth century many

21. George R. Knight, *Philosophy and Education: An Introduction in Christian Education Perspective* (Berrien Springs, Mich.: Andrews University Press, 1980), 164–65.

churches in the United States had shown social passivism and affirmed the status quo. This situation is changing as churches address social issues and become more actively involved in social, political, and economic action and witness.

Christians can affirm the salvation of groups of persons and structures to the extent that they conform to the revealed will of God. Standards of justice, righteousness, peace, truth, and love apply to human associations as well as to individual lives. Christians can recognize the need for a balance between a concern for personal salvation and a concern for the salvation of groups, communities, institutions, structures, and nations. This balance will be explored in chapter 2 in a discussion of the principle of conversion, which follows from a consideration of the realities of sin.

What part does education play in this process of salvation? Education is a vehicle for sharing the content of the faith and addressing the dimension of faith identified with the theological term *notitia*. This dimension deals with the intellectual understanding of the facts or *indicia* of Christ's life and work and the necessity of commitment to him for salvation. But content can include affective, psychomotor, and lifestyle content in addition to cognitive content.[23] Christian education intends to embrace the head, heart, hands, and way of life of participants. Christian education calls for a comprehensive vision for conversion that touches all of life. Chapter 2 will consider conversion as an organizing and comprehensive principle for Christian education.

The Present Ministry of the Holy Spirit

Christian educators maintain that the presence and work of the Holy Spirit is indispensable for effective educational ministry. Spirituality is a dimension of the life of persons and groups. Spiritual values impinge upon all Christian educational

22. Richard F. Lovelace, *Dynamics of Spiritual Life: An Evangelical Theology of Renewal* (Downers Grove, Ill.: InterVarsity, 1979), 112–14. See also Findley B. Edge, "The Evangelical Concern for Social Justice," *Religious Education* 74 (September–October 1979): 481–89.

23. James Michael Lee makes these distinctions in *The Content of Religious Education: A Social Science Approach* (Birmingham, Ala.: Religious Education Press, 1985).

31

efforts. The Holy Spirit is the Spirit of truth (John 15:26), and the Spirit guides the followers of Jesus into all truth (John 16:13). The Spirit's work was crucial in the origin of the Scriptures: "For prophecy never had its origin in the will of man, but men spoke from God as they were carried along by the Holy Spirit" (2 Pet. 1:21). This work of the Holy Spirit is designated "inspiration." In addition, the Holy Spirit has a crucial part in the understanding and teaching of God's Word, and this work is termed "illumination." Thus the Holy Spirit functions as the interpreter of the sacred Scriptures, and those who teach the Scriptures must consciously and intentionally depend upon the Holy Spirit to teach effectively and to influence the lives of students.

The Holy Spirit is also the active agent in equipping and filling Christian teachers to enable them to teach. Teaching is a spiritual gift that enables Christ's body, the church, to mature and to minister effectively. The proper exercise of the gift of teaching requires the continuous ministry of the Spirit to empower and guide teachers. Guidance and power are crucial if the lives of students are to be transformed and not merely informed by being confronted with the Word of God. The Holy Spirit also works in the lives of teachers to encourage a faithful stewardship of the gift of teaching itself.

In the study and life of students, the Holy Spirit's ministry brings about application and personal appropriation of the truths shared or discovered. This application and appropriation involves the cognitive, affective, intentional, and behavioral aspects of persons. Students need to gain an intellectual understanding of God's truths as revealed and discovered. This understanding is tempered by the recognition of the limitations of one's understanding and knowledge, along with an affirmation of that of which one can be certain. The Spirit's ministry involves transformation of the students' and the teachers' minds. In a similar way, the Holy Spirit renews the feelings, attitudes, intentions, motives, and actions of students. Students are called to submit to the Spirit's promptings that require obedience, to appreciate and love those values the Spirit indicates are after the heart of God, to respond in actions consistent with the Spirit's agenda, and to delight in the knowledge of God. The Holy Spirit also fosters a sense of mystery, wonder, and awe in

32

the lives of persons. These challenges posed for students must be shown in the lives of teachers to the end that both students and teachers may love God and their neighbors as themselves. The current interest in the spirituality of teaching must be related in Christian education to a consideration of the person and work of the Holy Spirit.[24] Spirituality is discussed in terms of Christian and cultural values in chapter 6.

The Resurrection of the Saved into Life and of the Unsaved into Damnation

Such a doctrine is not popular in an age of pluralism that stresses the need for tolerance and universal salvation for all persons. Nevertheless, biblical revelation describes the reality of God's judgment and wrath upon those who consciously reject salvation as offered in God's Son Jesus Christ. Judgment and wrath are not contrary to God's love, mercy, and justice, but are necessary complements to these other divine attributes. God's judgment and wrath are consistent with God's holiness and truthfulness. As this doctrine relates to Christian education, it implies human accountability to God's demands and expectations and consequences of human choice. Such a stance recognizes that much can be gained from ecumenical and interfaith dialogue and that God's gracious judgment is distinct from human evaluation and arrogance.

A dominant theme of modern Western life is the satisfaction of personal needs. Current educational wisdom advocates the clear identification of needs and careful design of teaching and learning to address those needs. Genuine educational needs must be addressed, but the implicit rationale of all education readily becomes the satisfaction of perceived needs. Abraham J. Heschel, a Jewish educator, warned about the dangers of such a perspective when he described the "tyranny of needs."[25] By this term, Heschel meant that in our culture needs have become

24. For further reading on the essential role of the Holy Spirit in Christian education, see Iris V. Cully, *Education for Spiritual Growth* (San Francisco: Harper and Row, 1984); Susanne Johnson, *Christian Spiritual Formation in the Church and Classroom* (Nashville: Abingdon, 1989); and Parker J. Palmer, *To Know as We Are Known: A Spirituality of Education* (San Francisco: Harper and Row, 1983).

33

holy, to the relative exclusion of considering God's demands and the responsibilities of persons before God. The satisfaction of one's personal needs, whatever their character, thus becomes a new form of idolatry. As a result, persons do not consider how they are needed by others and in a sense by God. This idea of being needed by God does not refute divine self-sufficiency or aseity, but challenges human self-satisfaction and self-sufficiency. Persons are confronted with their responsibility before God as God's creatures. Human responsibility can be discussed in two general areas. First, persons are responsible to God in all of life. Second, persons are responsible to God's creation, which includes other persons, the created world, and themselves. These responsibilities entail obligations, the fulfillment of which satisfies the deepest longings of the human heart to be needed and satisfied through service to God and others. This consideration of needs will again be raised in chapter 6 in a discussion of educational evaluation.

Christian educators are to help persons to be aware of their responsibilities and to enable them to fulfill these responsibilities by the grace of God. The task is to love God with all of one's heart, soul, mind, and strength, and one's neighbor as oneself. To fulfill this task, students need a vast knowledge and appreciation of God's special and general revelation and a willingness to come to terms with the implications of Christ's reign. Teachers and students are simultaneously humbled and inspired by the challenges of this task. In addition, they are assured of the grace of God in the person of Jesus Christ and in the indwelling presence of the Holy Spirit in order to accomplish the task.

The resurrection to life or damnation impresses upon each person the ultimate seriousness of one's calling and the final significance of one's choice in following after God or pursuing one's own way in life. This doctrine does not imply fatalism, despair, or futility. Rather, it resounds with hope for those who receive the grace of God in Jesus Christ. It also resounds with zeal to share the gospel of Jesus Christ with its multifaceted

25. Abraham J. Heschel, *Between God and Man: An Interpretation of Judaism from the Writings of Abraham Heschel*, ed. Fritz A. Rothschild (New York: Free Press, 1959), 129–51. Also see Victor Gross, *Educating to Reverence: The Legacy of Abraham Heschel* (Bristol, Ind.: Wyndham Hall, 1989).

implications for life. Christian educators share this vision of God's ultimate concern for creation and encourage the students' response to God's call for lives of obedience and joy in God's presence. The words of Jesus provide reassurance:

> Then Jesus declared, "I am the bread of life. He who comes to me will never go hungry, and he who believes in me will never be thirsty. But as I told you, you have seen me and still you do not believe. All that the Father gives me will come to me, and whoever comes to me I will never drive away. For I have come down from heaven not to do my will but to do the will of him who sent me. And this is the will of him who sent me, that I shall lose none of all that he has given me, but raise them up at the last day. For my Father's will is that everyone who looks to the Son and believes in him shall have eternal life, and I will raise him up at the last day." [John 6:35–40]

The Spiritual Unity of Believers in Our Lord Jesus Christ

The spiritual unity of all believers in Jesus Christ poses the challenge of ecumenical dialogue for evangelicals and the need to avoid arrogance in one's theological posture. This challenge does not negate the need to state and defend one's convictions while affirming an identity. But it does suggest the need to avoid a parochialism or sectarianism that refuses to recognize that one may be mistaken or that truth may be discerned by Christians from other theological persuasions. Spiritual unity suggests that all truth is God's truth and that God reserves the right to use those believers in Jesus Christ with whom we do not agree theologically, to use those who are not evangelical by theological persuasion. It is also possible to suggest that God's truths can be discerned and shared by persons from diverse theological perspectives. For example, God used Cornelius to teach Peter about God's comprehensive work of salvation (Acts 10).

This theological distinctive implies for Christian education that dialogue with Christians from diverse theological perspectives is needed if spiritual unity is to be explored and maintained. A second implication is that openness, along with the need for clarity in one's theological convictions, is required in any effort that is more than indoctrination or conditioning. Bal-

35

ancing freedom and form, or discipline and creativity, is a constant challenge in teaching. Spiritual unity is not realized at the cost of diversity, but in honoring the diversity present in God's creation and the new creation of the Christian church. Spiritual unity does not insist upon uniformity of religious expression and life in areas not revealed as normative for Christian faith. Too much Christian education has squelched the God-given creativity and the new possibilities with which God's Spirit has sought to bless humankind. Such creativity is not realized at the cost of the truth, and new possibilities must not be seen as negating the need for continuity along with change in the tasks of Christian education. Discerning and fostering spiritual unity is not an easy task, but requires the best efforts of each generation. In these efforts all must acknowledge the work of God's grace and the openness to receive the gift of unity that God alone has granted in Jesus Christ.

Principles that emerge from one's theology can provide landmarks for the journey of faith in the ministry of Christian education. This journey is not one without risk or adventure; this fact is to be celebrated. Each new generation must wrestle with the meaning and implications of these principles for practice without losing sight of God's high calling and the Christian vocation of educating in the faith. This apostolic faith has been delivered to us in the life, death, and resurrection of Jesus the Christ with the promise of God's continuing presence through the ministry of the Holy Spirit. Building upon these principles from the recent past, Christian educators are challenged to formulate a comprehensive model that will serve to address present and future generations. Chapter 2 will explore the theological concept of conversion as an organizing principle for Christian education within the evangelical heritage.

2

Principles for the Present and Future

In exploring principles for Christian education, evangelical educators must identify the biblical and theological distinctives of their tradition that have significance for the present and future. One such biblical and theological distinctive is the emphasis upon conversion.[1] In this chapter I expand upon traditional evangelical understandings of conversion to include a lifelong process that includes justification, sanctification, and edification along with the compre-

---

1. Mary C. Boys calls this distinctive evangelism in her analysis of contemporary approaches to religious education in the United States. She defines evangelism as "preaching and teaching the Scriptures in such a way to arouse conversion." (13). See her important work *Educating in Faith: Maps and Visions* (San Francisco: Harper and Row, 1989), 13–38, 111–19, 146–47. See also Boys, "Conversion as a Foundation of Religious Education," *Religious Education* 77 (March–April 1982): 211–24, in which she considers some of the implications of conversion in religious education. She argues for an understanding of conversion that is holistic and multidimensional, as is the case in this work. In *Educating in Faith*, Boys names three patterns in contemporary modifications of the approach of evangelism, which include transmission of the truth (which can be equated in my model with the task of proclamation); faith shared in a countercultural, apostolic community (equated with community and advocacy; and mission (equated with service and community). The one task that is not incorporated in Boys's analysis is that of worship and the experience of joy, which I place in the center of my model.

hensive tasks of the Christian church in relationship to educational ministries. For evangelicals this suggests that conversion can be a comprehensive and organizing principle for Christian education.

Evangelical Christians affirm the importance of conversion for persons to enter a living relationship with God. This interest in conversion has focused primarily on the individual response of persons to the call of Jesus Christ and their faith in the provision of salvation offered in his person and work. The Christian faith asserts that by the grace of God persons respond to the gifts of salvation and adoption and thus are incorporated into the family of God with all of the resulting privileges and responsibilities.[2] This is the good news that evangelicals delight to proclaim.

While this emphasis upon conversion is to be celebrated in a time when personal accountability and integrity are viewed as secondary concerns in society, it can too readily neglect a comprehensive appreciation of the breadth and depth of Christian conversion that is present in both personal and corporate life. To widen and deepen their appreciation of the full dimensions of the lordship of Jesus Christ, Christian educators must consider the nature and implications of conversion in their ministries. The term *Christian educators* refers to all Christians, clergy and laity, who educate both explicitly and implicitly through their lives and actions. In order to begin this consideration, all Christians must first explore the biblical foundation for conversion.

This exploration will provide an organizing principle for forming a comprehensive, holistic model of Christian education that integrates the various tasks of the church in a vital relationship with educational ministries. That key principle is conversion itself and its possibilities for individuals and communities. This evangelical concern for conversion may be compared with contemporary interest in transformation and liberation in other

2. For a fuller discussion of the theological distinctive of conversion among evangelical Christians, see Robert W. Pazmiño, *Foundational Issues in Christian Education: An Introduction in Evangelical Perspective* (Grand Rapids: Baker, 1988), 51–54. One recent example of a practical work that focuses on this distinctive is Ken Hemphill and R. Wayne Jones, *Growing an Evangelical Sunday School* (Nashville: Broadman, 1989). For a recent comprehensive study of conversion, see V. Bailey Gillespie, *The Dynamics of Religious Conversion: Identity and Transformation* (Birmingham, Ala.: Religious Education Press, 1991).

theological traditions. Conversion can provide a comprehensive principle that addresses not only the personal dimensions of faith and life, but the communal and societal dimensions as well. The current theological interest in both liberation and transformation with its particular focus on the community and society can be encompassed in a comprehensive vision of conversion that is faithful to biblical understandings.[3]

A Biblical Foundation

As John Marsh points out, in biblical usage conversion refers to the act of turning or returning. In the Hebrew Scriptures the term *sub*, which means "to turn back," can refer to God's turning to persons both favorably, as in Deuteronomy 13:17, where God is described as "turning" from anger to mercy and compassion, or negatively, as in Joshua 24:20, where the people of the nation of Israel are warned that if they forsake God and serve foreign gods, God will "turn" from them. Conversion also refers to people turning back to (*sub*) God, as in the case of Jeremiah 3:14, where people respond to God's choice, or away from God, as in Jeremiah 8:4–6, where they turn away and pursue their own course in life. In general, people turning from God is viewed as rebellion, whereas turning to God is viewed as the work of God's grace and human cooperation with it. This turning to God is "more than a change of mind, more than undergoing some experience; it is a concrete change to a new way of life."[4]

3. For an insightful analysis of conversion in the New Testament, see Beverly Roberts Gaventa, *From Darkness to Light: Aspects of Conversion in the New Testament* (Philadelphia: Fortress, 1986). Gaventa argues for at least three types of conversion: alternation, pendulum-like conversion, and transformation. She states, "Alternation occurs when change grows out of an individual's past behavior. It is the logical consequence of previous choices. Pendulum conversion involves the rejection of past convictions and affiliations for an affirmed present and future. Transformation applies to conversions in which a new way of perception forces the radical reinterpretation of the past. Here the past is not rejected but reconstructed as part of a new understanding of God and world" (148). The discussion of conversion in this chapter emphasizes pendulum conversion and transformation rather than alternation.

4. John Marsh, "Conversion," in *The Interpreter's Dictionary of the Bible*, ed. George A. Buttrick (Nashville: Abingdon, 1962), 678. See also John M. Mulder, "Conversion," in *Harper's Encyclopedia of Religious Education*, ed. Iris V. Cully and Kendig B. Cully (San Francisco: Harper and Row, 1990), 160–63.

In the New Testament the followers of Jesus were described as followers of "the Way" as a result of their conversions. Christians had turned from (*epistrepho*) a former way of living to embrace a new way in Jesus Christ. But it is important to note that the New Testament, as Marsh indicates, does not speak of God turning to persons. This is the case because the incarnation itself is the fulfillment of all such turning on the part of God. Though the word *conversion* is used to describe the act of turning away from (*epistrepho*), as in Galatians 4:9, it is most often used for persons turning to God (Acts 9:35; 15:19). True turning to God incorporates the three experiences of repentance, belief, and faith. Repentance is turning from sin to God, which involves a change of mind and a corresponding feeling of remorse or regret for one's past disobedience. Repentance ushers us into a new way of life. Belief is the content we affirm about God and the human condition in relation to God. Faith focuses upon Jesus with whom we walk and, in conversion, leads not only to a new way of life for persons of faith, but to a spiritual transformation as well.[5]

One question from New Testament sources relative to conversion is whether radical or gradual conversion is in view. A decision with regard to this issue will influence one's philosophy of and approach to Christian education in relation to conversion. The so-called Pauline paradigm as described by Luke in Acts 9:1–19, 22:1–21, and 26:1–23 emphasizes conversion as an event that is radical and life-transforming in nature. This Pauline paradigm has been stressed in evangelism and evangelization, but a careful consideration of his conversion suggests that even Paul gained a fuller experience of his conversion over time (Gal. 1:15–19).

A distinct paradigm that has not received as much interest is what can be termed the Petrine or Markan paradigm for conversion. Peter's conversion can be viewed as a process that is explicit with his confession, near the town of Caesarea Phillipi, that Jesus was the Messiah (Matt. 16:13–19). As C. Ellis Nelson observes, "Peter was the first disciple to understand the divine mission of Jesus, and to whatever extent we can say a person is saved when making a confession, Peter is that per-

5. Marsh, "Conversion."

40

son."[6] This same Peter was used mightily by God in preaching on the day of Pentecost, and yet he was not thoroughly converted because his understanding of the gospel did not include a place for the Gentiles. This awareness, a more thorough and radical conversion, is revealed in Acts 10, where Peter is confronted by God and Cornelius to embrace a dimension of the gospel of which he was previously unaware. Peter in the Lukan interpretation was converted to a more inclusive understanding of the Christian community when he baptized the first Gentile convert to the Christian faith. This second conversion correlates with the second task of the church, koinonia, which will be discussed later. Nelson points out that Peter was already converted under the teaching of Jesus, and he was the human founder and recognized leader of the church; yet not all areas of his inner self were converted. Peter had been formed as a Jew, and this early training remained after his conversion at Caesarea Phillipi. It required a unique second encounter with God to break the formations of Peter's youth and to transform his mind so that he could see the gospel in a new light.[7]

In an analysis that is similar to Nelson's insights, Richard Peace proposes that the unifying theme in the Gospel of Mark is the unfolding conversion of the twelve apostles as they discover, stage by stage, who Jesus is. He argues that this paradigm of conversion as a process must be given equal weight with the Pauline paradigm of conversion as an event.[8] Thus biblical warrant exists for a broader understanding of conversion that can include both radical and gradual elements of transformations as persons encounter God. The Reformed theologian Herman Bavinck came to affirm this broader understanding of conversion when he maintained that the Christian needs two conversions: one away from the world to Jesus Christ, and the other in

6. C. Ellis Nelson, *How Faith Matures* (Louisville: Westminster/John Knox, 1989), 112.

7. Ibid., 113.

8. Richard Peace, "The Conversion of the Twelve: A Study of the Process of Conversion in the New Testament," Ph.D. diss., University of Natal, South Africa, 1990. Peace discusses conversion in terms of the three movements or phases of insight, turning, and transformation, and he argues for a holistic understanding of conversion as a process.

the name of Christ back to the world.[9] Such a broadened under-standing of conversion is also warranted on the basis of the accounts of persons who have experienced conversion.[10] In this chapter I argue the case for multiple turnings in which these transformations relate to the five distinct tasks of the Christian church.

In summarizing the insights gained from the biblical concept of conversion, Orlando E. Costas observed:

> First, conversion means a turning from sin (and self) to God (and God's work). Second, this act involves a change of mind, which implies the abandonment of an old world view and the adoption of a new one. Third, conversion entails a new allegiance, a new trust, and a new life commitment. Fourth, conversion is but the beginning of a new journey and carries implicitly the seed of new turns. Fifth, conversion is surrounded by the redemptive love of God as revealed in Jesus Christ and witnessed to by the Holy Spirit.[11]

Conversion thus suggests a radical reorientation for persons that requires centering all of life upon the will and reign of God. God's reign embraces not only the personal dimension of life,

9. As cited in N. H. Beversluis, *Toward a Theology of Education: Occasional Papers from Calvin College,* vol. 1, no. 1, February 1981, 19.

10. See the work of Hugh T. Kerr and John M. Mulder, ed., *Conversions: The Christian Experience* (Grand Rapids: Eerdmans, 1983), for an account of the experience of various persons in relation to their conversion.

11. Orlando E. Costas, *Liberating News: A Theology of Contextual Evangelization* (Grand Rapids: Eerdmans, 1989), 113. For a full discussion of the call to conversion see chapter 6 of this work, which describes conversion as a series of new challenges, new turnings, and new experiences that are rooted in Christ and expressed in a distinctive quality of life. Bernard Lonergan provides a similar analysis in *Method in Theology* (New York: Herder and Herder, 1972), 130–31. He sees conversion normally as a prolonged process, though its explicit acknowledgment may be concentrated in a few momentous judgments and decisions. Rather than a series of developments, conversion is a change of course and direction in life that leads to a new and distinct world and a new relationship with history, one's community, and one's culture. For a discussion of Lonergan's work in relation to religious education, see Thomas H. Groome, "Conversion, Nurture and Educators," *Religious Education* 76 (September–October 1981): 482–96. Gaventa, in *From Darkness to Light,* states that "conversion brings new life (John 3:1–7), a transformed mind (Rom. 12:1–2), a new community (Acts 11:1–18), a new perspective (Phil. 3:2–11)" (152).

but also the communal and societal dimensions where the effects of God's reign may not be as readily discerned and addressed. Conversion implies that the center for life exists in the triune God and that persons at every point in their lives move in ways that are either directed toward that center or away from that center. Therefore it is possible to conceive that a person who has been "converted" at some earlier point in life may now be moving in directions that do not center upon God. Likewise, it is possible to conceive of a person who has not been "converted" (as perceived by the Christian community) moving in a direction that is centered upon God. This possibility theologians call "prevenient grace," a term that describes the work of God and the response of persons prior to the point of conscious and public conversion.[12]

A similar analysis can be suggested for both communities and societies, and is certainly warranted in the light of the teaching of Matthew 25:31–46, where the focus for judgment includes the works of the nations, and of the teaching of Revelation 2 and 3, where the focus for judgment is the works of various Christian communities or churches. Both nations and local communities are evaluated on the basis of the direction of their lives and actions, either centered on God or centered upon other gods. The apostle Paul described this choice to the Christians at Rome as worshiping and serving the Creator or worshiping and serving created things (Rom. 1:25). Thus societies, communities, and individuals constantly must decide whether they will center their lives upon God and choose life, or center their lives upon idols and choose death. Such terms grate on modern sensitivities, but such a stance was not uncommon to the prophetic tradition found in the Scriptures. This stance does not deny the existence of many complex areas of our lives where the choice between life and death is not readily apparent or easily resolved. But it does recognize the need to struggle with how our personal and corporate lives embody or deny the reality of our conversion, the reality of our turning to God in response to the grace revealed in Jesus the Christ. This stance

12. For a basic discussion of prevenient grace, see T. C. Hammond, *In Understanding Be Men: An Introductory Handbook on Christian Doctrine* (Downers Grove, Ill.: InterVarsity, 1936), 136–37.

also affirms the need of Christian educators to assess their efforts in relation to the radical demands of Christian conversion, which are to embrace all of life. In order to address this challenge, educators must name and claim a vision that embraces a comprehensive understanding of conversion and holds forth the possibility of new turnings in the walk of faith.

Prologomena for a Comprehensive Vision of Conversion and Education

Building upon a biblical concept and principle of conversion, Christian educators must conceive of Christian education in a way that links theory and practice to the primary tasks of the church. Without such a linkage any discussion of conversion can remain just an intellectual exercise. To explore the linkage, I propose a working definition of Christian education and suggest its implications in relation to one model for the tasks of the church.

Christian education can be defined as the process of sharing or gaining distinctives of the Christian story and truth (information) and Christian values, attitudes, and lifestyle (formation), and fostering the change of persons, communities, societies, and structures (transformation) by the power of the Holy Spirit to a fuller expression of God's reign in Jesus Christ. This process requires the partnership of God with people who are called and gifted to teach and it requires openness of all persons to the possibility of conversion or transformation. This definition incorporates the three essential elements or foci of education, namely, content, persons, and the context of community and society, along with the dynamics of information, formation, and transformation.[13] By incorporating the three essential elements we may call this definition trinitarian.

13. For further discussion of these points see Pazmiño, *Foundational Issues,* 111–13. Ronald Habermas has suggested that this definition is paralleled in Paul's summative testimony of the Way in Acts 24:14–16 in the following three points: content is expressed in Paul's belief in the "law and prophets" (v. 14), and especially the resurrection (v. 15); the formation of persons is present in the shape of Paul's resultant "hope" (v. 15) and worship as a life response (v. 14); and the transformation of the community/society is suggested in both the vertical and horizontal dimensions of a clear conscience (v. 16). Thus these three verses serve as a summary of the Christian walk of faith.

44

A comprehensive vision of Christian education will elaborate upon this educational trinity of content, persons, and context, recognizing that people learn content in the context of their community and society. Exclusive emphasis on one or even two of these elements does not foster a comprehensive vision and can result in a truncated practice. The history of educational thought and practice reveals that advocates have often disproportionately stressed one of these elements, resulting in limited possibilities for participants and an inappropriate reductionism.[14] Such reductionism promoted an educational idolatry rather than embraced the whole counsel of God. The quality of education resulting from a less than comprehensive vision can affect the life of a community and society for generations, as the history of Christian education evidences.[15] A similar danger exists for Christian educators who do not explicitly or implicitly relate their efforts of teaching and learning to the five principal tasks of the Christian church and the corresponding forms of conversion that can be proposed in relation to these tasks. This analysis also suggests that pastors must understand and assume their responsibilities as teachers, as religious educators in their congregations, and must undergird the efforts of others in the congregation who have gifts for teaching. The responsibility of teaching is expected of all who would serve as leaders in the church, who are described as being "apt to teach" (1 Tim. 3:2; 2 Tim. 2:24).[16]

The Five-Task Model

It is possible to envision the five principal tasks of the church in terms of a web or a network. This web can be drawn as a cir-

14. The nature of this reductionism is discussed in chapter 6.
15. A helpful introduction to this history is provided by Marianne Sawicki, *The Gospel in History: Portrait of a Teaching Church, The Origins of Christian Education* (New York: Paulist, 1988).
16. For further study regarding the role of the pastor in the educational ministry of the church, see Earl E. Shelp and Ronald H. Sunderland, eds., *The Pastor as Teacher* (New York: Pilgrim, 1989); Robert L. Browning, *The Pastor as Religious Educator* (Birmingham, Ala.: Religious Education Press, 1989); and Clark M. Williamson and Ronald J. Allen, *The Teaching Minister* (Louisville: Westminster/John Knox, 1991).

Figure 2
The Five-Task Model

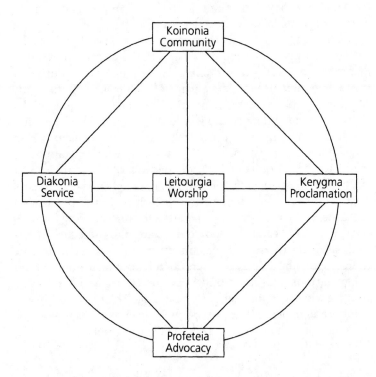

cle with four points or tasks on the circumference and the fifth task as the hub or center (see fig. 2).

The four tasks on the circle include call and commitment (*kerygma*), community and covenant (*koinonia*), care and concern (*diakonia*), conscience and challenge (*propheteia*), and celebration and creativity (*leitourgia*). Other terms that can be applied to these five tasks are proclamation, community, service, advocacy, and worship. The metaphor of a web suggests that these five tasks must be intimately connected if a full understanding, appreciation, and expression of conversion is to be nurtured in the educational ministry of the church. In relation to each of the points on the web, Christians can experience conversion and Christian education can foster such experiences. This model does not suggest that Christian educators can effectuate conversion, which is the work of the Holy Spirit alone in the lives of persons, communities, and societies. But it does suggest that those called and equipped to teach share the possibility of conversion to life under God's reign. The organizing and comprehensive principle of conversion has implications for the ongoing life and mission of the Christian church.

Kerygma

One major task in the ministries of Christian education is sharing the Christian story and enabling others to appropriate that story in relation to their lives. In the proclamation of what is true about God, persons, and the world, Christians must emphasize the place of choice, commitment, and a personal response to the call of God. In a biblical sense, knowing God means to respond with mind, heart, and actions to the good news declared by God and God's spokespersons. In this knowing, occasioned by the proclamation of the gospel, persons are willing to stake their lives on the new life offered to them in Jesus Christ. José Miguez Bonino has said that the goal of sharing the Christian faith is to elicit not only knowing in a cognitive sense alone, but also faithful obedience to the will of God.[17]

An example of this task of kerygma is the deliberate effort in Sunday school and elsewhere to tell the stories of Jesus and all of Scripture to persons across the life span. The challenge in telling or discovering the stories as Susanne Johnson suggests, is to connect the Christian story with the lives and cultural stories of today's participants.[18] Telling the Christian story includes evangelism or outreach, because in the telling a response and commitment is expected. The telling implies an invitation to make the story one's own and to live out the implications of embracing the story.

From this perspective Christian education is a matter of choice and commitment in which people are confronted with

17. José Miguez Bonino, *Doing Theology in a Revolutionary Situation* (Philadelphia: Fortress, 1975), 87.
18. Susanne Johnson, *Christian Spiritual Formation in the Church and Classroom* (Nashville: Abingdon, 1989), 90.

God's view of the human situation and the clear, definite call to repent and be converted (Mark 1:15; Acts 2:38–39). This call to conversion is issued on the basis of the work of Jesus Christ and the gift of salvation is offered to those who respond in faith. Such an offer is based upon the grace of God, but demands a new life to be lived in allegiance to God's will for all of creation. The initial turning to God in response to Jesus Christ has traditionally been termed conversion, but implied is a predisposition to additional turnings that may be required and in fact anticipated in beginning a new journey with God. The educational task in relation to kerygma is to share the information about God, Jesus Christ, and our human dilemma necessary for persons to grasp what is both offered to them and demanded of them in a call to conversion. What is offered is a new life in Christ, and what is demanded is willingness to die to one's old life. Persons of all ages need time and space to grapple with the implications of the call of God upon their lives and their commitments. This grappling must be done in dialogue with others within the Christian community, which leads us to consider the place of koinonia.

Koinonia

The issue of conversion in koinonia is turning from a life centered upon oneself or upon one's family or group to a life that centers upon a community defined in terms that break all of the barriers normally associated with humanity. As the apostle Paul declared in Galatians 3:28: "There is neither Jew nor Greek, slave nor free, male nor female, for you are all one in Christ Jesus." With Christ there is no longer any place for the religious, cultural, linguistic, sexual, and social distinctions that have alienated and divided persons, communities, and societies. A community redefined in Christ affirms the worth and dignity of every person. The promise for all people, whatever their background or standing, is the possibility of being joined to a new community of God, namely, the Christian church. The strength of the individual Christian is fostered by being in community with other Christians who practice mutual edification.

Among those who came to appreciate this new understanding of community include the apostles Peter and Paul. Peter came to embrace a Gentile, Cornelius, as a fellow member of the body of Christ and as a brother with full rights and standing in the community of faith. Paul, as an apostle to the Gentiles, also came to embrace an understanding of slaves that required their masters to treat them as brothers and sisters in Christ. The barrier between slave and free was broken in this new perspective from the New Testament Book of Philemon and eventually the institution of slavery itself was questioned, as Christians came to see the radical implications of what Christ had accomplished. These examples of Paul and Peter are all the more remarkable in the light of the fact that the first-century Jewish male regularly gave thanks to God in worship that he was not born a Gentile or a woman. In addition, Jews of the first century had much contempt for slavery and slaves. This suggests that both Peter and Paul were converted from their previous understanding of community (one that was exclusive) to a new covenant of grace (one that was inclusive of all persons who placed their faith in Jesus Christ). This new covenant implied that the Christian community is to be diverse but unified in Jesus Christ.

The contemporary struggle of various persons to gain their full privileges in the Christian community points out the need to see conversion as a continuous process in the life of the church and society. The educational task in relation to koinonia is to foster a sense of community that encourages and empowers people to live interdependently with God, with other Christians (both globally and locally), with humanity in its amazing religious plurality, and with the entire creation. Such a perspective embraces a conversion from the numerous parochial and tribal associations that characterize communal and societal life to a cosmic and universal appreciation of the Christian community. The Christian community welcomes individuals who are different in their race, class, gender, status, power, and culture to become disciples of Jesus the Christ.

Given the multiple divisions that plague the global community, the conversion suggested for koinonia is no less radical than that related to kerygma. As in the first century, today there is to be neither black nor white in South Africa or the United States, neither Catholic nor Protestant in Northern Ireland, neither Sandinista nor Contra in Nicaragua when Christians gather and where such distinctions undermine an essential unity. How is this possible? It is one of the marvels of the Christian faith to overcome the distance between individuals, communities, and societies. A conversion is needed. I had a personal glimpse of what such a conversion to koinonia embodies when I went fishing one day with my father and son at Canarsie Pier in Brooklyn, New York. People from every racial, ethnic, and cultural group represented in the city of New York were fishing together that day. Women and men, girls and boys of all ages were fishing, and a sense of harmony and community existed among those people assembled on a hot, sun-drenched summer day. Everyone shared in the activity and enjoyment of fishing. People shared their fishing bait, their fishing advice, their fishing stories, and even themselves in an amazing way. This was just one small illustration of what Jesus intended for his followers and what God intends for those called into the new reign of Jesus Christ. This new reign also includes a distinctive call to serve, which leads to a consideration of diakonia.

Diakonia

Diakonia embodies the answer to the question: For what purpose are persons converted? In an ultimate sense the answer is, "To glorify and enjoy God forever." But in a penultimate sense the answer is the care and concern of the whole people of God for the needs of individuals, societies, and the world. The apostle Paul suggests this in Ephesians 2:8–10: "For it is by grace you have been saved, through faith—and this not from yourselves, it is the gift of God—not by works, so that no one can boast. For we are God's workmanship, created in Christ Jesus to do good works, which God prepared in advance for us to do." Doing good works requires that all Christians identify with a pastoral calling. Such a calling is not limited to the clergy, but includes the laity in mission and ministry.

The educational task in relation to diakonia is fostering the connection of one's faith to acts of service. Christians must understand that knowledge of the Christian faith implies a willingness and a predisposition to serve in whatever capacity will meet the overwhelming needs that exist. Exposure to realities in developing countries—that a widening gap between the rich and the poor intensifies the needs of the poor—can move us toward a new commitment to Christian service. Even in the United States, considered one of the richest countries in the world, we must choose whether we will accept the responsibility to care for the poor, as we have done in the past. The option of caring for the poor does not eliminate the need for ministry at all socioeconomic levels, but it poses a question of how we allocate increasingly limited resources.

One example of how a program in Christian education can be "turned" around in relation to diakonia comes from an adult Sunday school class that met in a local church in Massachusetts. Class members decided that their weekly discussion of the Christian faith required some joint expression of service. Class members decided to hold monthly "barn-raising" events—work projects one Saturday of each month—in which class members, their families, and any other interested persons could participate. Projects included repairing a roof, cleaning out an attic and cellar in the home of an older adult who could not do the work, repairing rooms needed for a shelter for battered women and their children, and disposing of refuse from an inner-city facility for the homeless. People were free to participate in whatever capacity they could. Each work project was followed up with a potluck dinner, a dessert time, and a time for singing, fellowship, and prayer. Individuals who could not do the work were welcome to the dinner, dessert, or fellowship time.

Through their experience of service together this group of initially loosely associated adults became a closely knit group that addressed important issues of their faith when they gathered for Sunday school and reflected upon their experiences of serving others. Class members experienced a corporate conversion in relating their faith to needs within their community that otherwise would not have been addressed. More than one individual turned to a new understanding and appreciation of the place of service in the Christian life. The class developed a sense of corporate and cooperative responsibilities. Much more was accomplished through joint efforts than individuals could accomplish serving alone. The witness provided to observers at the work sites also took on a different character with the example of many workers. Class members also experienced a conversion to an activist style of life called for by the gospel, which is witnessed to by deeds as well as by words. At some points in life an activist style implies advocacy in the area of social witness for the gospel in relation to the task of *propheteia.*

Propheteia

The prophetic task of the church has not been readily owned or nurtured in recent history in the United States. This suggests that the Christian church has too readily accommodated the faith to the dominant culture, and that Christians have assimilated a highly materialistic and individualized lifestyle. As Christians we have an advocate, the Lord Jesus Christ, who represents us (1 John 2:1). We as Christians must stand up for those who may not have an advocate. Advocacy also involves naming the idols of our own personal and corporate lives and proposing alternatives that are in harmony with God's interests for humanity and all of creation. By addressing our personal and corporate idols we are able to respond to the needs of others and to serve as advocates.

The gospel affirms the place of denunciation as well as annunciation. The cry for justice and human rights can challenge Christians to express their social love by advocating for those who are oppressed and to live a Christian lifestyle. In the United States we need to scrutinize the ethics of not adequately supporting education and Christian education, for this failure relates to the development of our greatest resource, namely, individuals created in the image of God. This situation requires critical evaluation in terms of Christian values and social witness.

The educational task in propheteia is to make people understand how commitment to God's reign relates to the dominant virtues and ideals of one's community or society. Points of convergence or complementarity between gospel virtues and ideals and those of one's culture are to be celebrated and conserved. But points of divergence and conflict require Christians to protest and to struggle with the possibility of transformation or conversion. Christians have their first allegiance to a Christian culture (Heb. 11:13), and in relation to propheteia they are persons of hope who are willing to stake their lives on the

52

changes that God can bring to fruition in their society. These changes require the work of the Holy Spirit at all levels of personal and corporate life and the willingness of Christians to accept their responsibilities as being in but not of the world.

An example of this task comes from my ministry in East Harlem, New York. In the effort to relate the parable of the good Samaritan during a children's church program, the youth of the church and I organized a walking tour of the community. As a result of the awareness raised in the youth, they themselves organized a summer outreach effort to neighborhood children that required their participation in a week-long training program as preparation. A number of those youth are now young adults and are actively involved in community efforts, lay and clerical, to advocate for the needs of various persons. A few have pursued Christian social ministry in regional and national organizations.

The conversion suggested in this prophetic task of the church requires risk and vulnerability, as exemplified by the Hebrew prophets. But to avoid risk is to deny the prophethood of all believers implied in the ministry of reconciliation (2 Cor. 5:16–21). Christians are called to reconcile their personal and corporate world to God, which requires holding forth the possibility of conversion, of turning, where it is needed. Conversion implies the denunciation of former realities where they are not faithful to God and the annunciation of new possibilities in Jesus Christ that embrace the totality of creation. The prophets of old assumed this task of calling peoples and nations to account before God, and Christians today must not shrink from such a demand. In prophetic ministry the ever-present dangers are those of burnout and the loss of perspective. Only in relation to a sustained life of worship and celebration safeguarded through the place of sabbath can Christians renew their strength and gain perspective. This is the task of leitourgia, from which we derive our understanding of liturgy, namely, the work of the whole people of God in worship.

Leitourgia

The final task of the church, which marks its distinctive role now and through eternity, is that of worship. Worship includes celebration and the expression of creativity that gives glory to God. This task is placed at the hub of the circle in my model to designate its priority and its potentially integrative function in the church. It is in relation to worship that people can experience the joy that God intends for all of creation through the redemption made possible in Jesus Christ and the presence of the Holy Spirit. Such an experience, though heightened in corporate worship, is not limited to that occasion. A sense of worship and of God's presence can encompass all of life, whenever two or three are gathered in the name of Jesus or individuals encounter God through their personal devotional life or in the marketplace.

Much of life in this world forces preoccupation with all that is created, with little or no time held sacred for an interest in the Creator. This preoccupation is broken only when people choose to break from it, and to do so does not presume a relocation of persons from everyday activities, demands, and contexts. But it does require willingness to encounter God in the ordinary affairs and interactions of life. Yet in order to gain such an appreciation, individuals also need to have a place for sabbath in their lives. The designation of sacred time and space signals an openness to be recreated and refreshed by God's grace in subsequent conversions. It also reaffirms that persons are created by God, and because created in God's image, are themselves creative. Here then people can be empowered by God to use their diverse creative abilities and energies for the glory of God.

Illustrations of this task emerge from a local mainline denominational church that takes seriously adult education for public worship. On occasion, this educational program involves people of all ages in quarterly events. The most significant sessions included one that focused on the history of baptism through the art and symbols associated with baptism, many of which are present in the sanctuary itself. A second session explored the church's hymnody and included many opportunities to sing together. The result was increased appreciation of the history and meaning of the hymns. A third session took place on Earth Day and celebrated the creation. Various learning centers were planned and directed by children in Sunday school. The children then actively engaged adults in a host of learning activities, often pairing a child and an adult. Many who participated gained a new appreciation of the creation as God's gift to humanity. This sense of God's gift was coordinated with that Sunday's themes of corporate worship.

Worship provides the opportunity for people to see life from God's perspective and to have their lives transformed as a result. Our chief end in life is to enjoy and glorify God. Worship provides the necessary time and place for people of all ages to gather and interact with a clear focus upon enjoying and glorifying God. The corporate nature of public worship enables us to sense and acknowledge a presence and power beyond human circumstances and limitations. That presence and power is God, who both invites and demands our attention, love, and life. By centering upon God, we may gain perspective on the particulars of our personal and corporate lives and by the work of the Holy Spirit we may integrate and make whole those particulars.

The educational task in relation to leitourgia is fostering a sense of worship that encompasses all of life and exploring avenues for integration through creative expression. An educational program that gives participants opportunity to express their creativity will also foster a sense of celebration and provide occasions for worship. In addition, a conversion is implied in enabling persons to incorporate the place of sabbath in their personal and corporate life. Sabbath is where the demands of life can be seen in a new perspective, the perspective of a recreated life in Christ. In the frenzied pace of modern life, fulfilling this task calls for a radical conversion in response to the gospel.

Conclusion

Orlando Costas has aptly observed that conversion requires new turnings throughout one's life because conversion continues to be needed until the consummation of God's reign.[19] In this chapter I have argued for an understanding of the principle of conversion that is multiple in character and comprehensive in scope. This multiple character of conversion embraces all the dimensions of personal and corporate life with a new way, a

19. Costas, *Liberating News*, 116.

new perspective instituted in Christ. The comprehensive scope of the conversion principle touches each of the various tasks of the church, which have been described as proclamation, community, service, advocacy, and worship. This stress upon the process of conversion is to complement the traditional emphasis in evangelical theology: that conversion is a radical event. Conversion is both an event and a process in relation to Christian education and the five-task model.

This five-task model can be compared with the contemporary approaches to Christian education identified by Jack Seymour and Donald Miller:[20] religious instruction, faith community, spiritual development, liberation, and interpretation. The approach of religious instruction stresses proclamation of the Christian faith; faith community stresses community; spiritual development stresses worship in all of life; liberation stresses service and advocacy; and interpretation stresses the connective framework between the five tasks, but particularly among proclamation, community, and worship. Opting for one of these five contemporary approaches can easily mean that we fail to see the bigger picture and all the necessary connections. But the five-task model can connect and integrate insights from the five contemporary models named by Seymour and Miller.

As a result of understanding conversion in terms of the five-task model, Christian educators are challenged to relate their efforts to the possibility of conversion throughout the lifespan of persons, communities, and societies. They are also challenged to reflect the ongoing nature of conversion itself in their own theory and practice. With such a challenge in mind Bernard Lonergan, a Roman Catholic theologian, has described conversion as three-dimensional:

> It is intellectual inasmuch as it regards our orientation to the intelligible and the true. It is moral inasmuch as it regards our orientation to the good. It is religious inasmuch as it regards our orientation to God. The three dimensions are dis-

20. For a discussion of these approaches see Jack L. Seymour and Donald E. Miller, eds., *Contemporary Approaches to Christian Education* (Nashville: Abingdon, 1982), chap. 1; and Jack L. Seymour and Donald E. Miller, eds., *Theological Approaches to Christian Education* (Nashville: Abingdon, 1990), chap. 1.

tinct, so that conversion can occur in one dimension without occurring in the other two, or in two dimensions without occurring in the other one. At the same time, the three dimensions are solidary. Conversion in one leads to conversion in the other dimensions, and relapse from one prepares for relapse from the others. . . The authentic Christian strives for the fullness of intellectual, moral and religious conversion. Without intellectual conversion he tends to misapprehend not only the world mediated by meaning, but also the word God has spoken within that world. Without moral conversion he tends to pursue not what truly is good, but what only apparently is good. Without religious conversion he is radically desolate: in the world without hope and without God (Ephes. 2:12).[21]

It is toward the fullness of conversion, intellectual, moral, and religious, that Christian educators must strive today and it is the principle of conversion in relation to the various tasks of the church that provides a holistic model for the present and the future. The connection between each of the five tasks of the church (proclamation, community, service, advocacy, and worship) and their interrelationships remains to be explored (chap. 4, which considers the topic of educational content). But prior to such consideration, Christian educators must relate their practice to the web of educational structures in which they serve and to the possible connections between the efforts of the Christian church and other structures. In these structures Christian educators must strive to be faithful to the organizing and comprehensive principle of conversion in their practice.

21. Bernard Lonergan, *Doctrinal Pluralism* (Milwaukee: Marquette University Press, 1971), 34–35.

3

Educational Structures

Because persons are not educated alone or outside of their context, we must eventually address the structural realities of education in communal or corporate life. These educational structures include social agencies and groups whose primary tasks are to pass on and to reform a body of knowledge, values, culture, and life to the next generations and to protect the ongoing character of social life. Individuals can be self-directed in their learning and interact with these social structures of education in distinct or unique ways. But even the most solitary or introspective individuals need to acknowledge the influence of others upon their lives. For example, reading a book whose author has long since died or even a recluse's life can be cited as social influences that have some relationship to social structures. These structures can be named even if they represent an alternative to societal norms for social interaction and relationships. How then can educators make sense of social and educational structures and provide insights for participants in educational programs for their relationships to and within such structures?

The Brazilian educator Paulo Freire calls attention to this social character of education when he affirms the three assumptions about effective education that he termed "conscientization": No one can teach anyone else; no one learns alone; and people learn together, acting in and on their world.[1] No one can teach anyone else in the sense that a person must be open to learn before a teacher can effectively teach. Such an openness to learn or a teachable spirit is required in the home, the church, the community, the school, and the workplace.[2] This first assumption permits the possibility of self-initiated and self-directed learning. A teacher may impose some content upon a student, but it certainly will not be owned, retained, or transferred to new situations without some level of active participation and cooperation. Thus guaranteed or secured learning occurs only when persons can assert that they have taught themselves something. But this assertion is further qualified by Freire's second assumption—that no one learns alone.

Learning takes place in a social context that presumes the presence and participation of other persons. Learning also presumes some content, which itself is a social product and is encoded in a symbol system. The symbol system also is a social product. Therefore, other persons are present either explicitly or implicitly in the learning experience. Learning cannot be a solitary process divorced from the social connections of life. Within the United States we have too often ignored the communal, social, and structural character of life. By doing so, we have failed to make the connections and linkages needed to gain a sense of the whole of life and the interdependence of the human community. Individualism has been stressed, to the detriment of developing strong community relationships.

Freire's third assumption, that people learn together as they act in and on their world, reaffirms the social aspect of educa-

1. Noel E. McGinn, "The Psycho-Social Method of Paulo Freire: Some Lessons from Experience," in *Inter-American Seminar on Literacy in Social and Economic Development* (New York: World Education, 1973), 10. "Conscientization" is better termed "problem-posing" or "transforming education," given the tendency to divorce action from consciousness-raising in the context of western society. Freire's commitment is to relate education to personal and corporate activity in the world and to transform those realities which do not promote human freedom.

2. For a discussion of a teachable spirit see Richard R. Osmer, *A Teachable Spirit: Recovering the Teaching Office in the Church* (Louisville: Westminster/John Knox, 1990).

tion. The human social fabric has been woven since the creation. Despite efforts in recent history to stress radical individualism rather than the corporate dimensions of life, the social character of life and the need for community have persisted. People need to recognize and embrace the "together" or "connected" quality of life and work for its enhancement. This is a particular challenge for educators.

The social or communal quality of created life is modeled for the human community by the divine community of Creator, Redeemer, and Sustainer, or in traditional language, Father, Son, and Holy Spirit. Being created in God's image and being in the world as God's creation requires sensitivity to the interdependent nature of spiritual and ecological life.

Formal, Nonformal, and Informal Education

In exploring the nature of educational structures, which are one form of social structure, Christian educators since the 1960s have discussed the differences between formal, informal, and nonformal education. This discussion has reflected a new appreciation of the diverse ways in which people are educated outside the experience of schooling or formal education. Prior to the 1960s any discussion of the history of education focused on the place of schools and the impact of schooling, assuming that the primary structure for education was the school. This focus is quite understandable because the clear societal commitment and investment of educational resources was in primary, secondary, and postsecondary schools in the United States. This was generally true throughout the northern hemisphere.

With the pioneering work of both Bernard Bailyn and Lawrence A. Cremin, historians of education and educators who were interested in the totality of education and lifelong education, a major shift in perspective occurred that defined education in terms much broader than a narrow focus upon schooling.[3] This expanded understanding resulted in recognition of other social

3. For an introduction to this broadened perspective see Bernard Bailyn, *Education in the Forming of American Society: Needs and Opportunities for Study* (New York: Norton, 1960); and Lawrence A. Cremin, *Traditions of American Education* (New York: Basic, 1976).

structures and groups that had a major impact upon education beyond its formal expressions. In fact, this new awareness resulted in a rereading of the earlier history of education and a recognition of the relative place of schools alongside the contributions of such social agencies as the family, the community, and the economy. The definition of education also shifted to include the learning gained from socialization, enculturation, and experiences outside of traditional classrooms. During the 1960s "free schools" and "schools without walls" were alternatives to formal and traditional settings. The extent of reaction to formal schooling was captured in the rise of "deschoolers" and personified in the works of Ivan Illich, John Holt, Jonathan Kozol, A. S. Neill, and Neil Postman, among others.[4]

In distinguishing formal, nonformal, and informal education it is helpful to conceive of these forms along a continuum with formal and informal education representing the opposing poles, and nonformal education at the midpoint of the continuum (see fig. 3).

Comparative educators P. Coombs and M. Ahmed have offered insight in defining these three general forms. Formal education is defined as that form of education that is institutionalized, chronologically graded, and hierarchically structured in a system that spans primary through higher education and could include even preschooling systems in some countries. Informal education is the lifelong process by which every person acquires and accumulates knowledge, skills, and insights from daily experiences and exposure to the environment and through interactions in life. Nonformal education is defined as any organized systematic educational activity carried on outside the framework of the formal system to provide selective types of learning to particular subgroups in the population. The distinction between informal and nonformal education rests with the motivation and goals of the individuals involved, and that between nonformal and formal education rests with the degree

4. See Ivan Illich, *Deschooling Society* (New York: Harper and Row, 1970); John Holt, *Freedom and Beyond* (New York: Dell, Laurel ed., 1972); Jonathan Kozol, *Free Schools* (Boston: Houghton Mifflin, 1972); A. S. Neill, *Summerhill: A Radical Approach to Child Rearing* (New York: Hart, 1960); and Neil Postman and Charles Weingartner, *Teaching as Subversive Activity* (New York: Delacorte, 1969).

Figure 3
Forms of Education

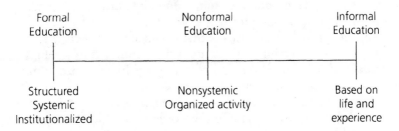

Formal Education	Nonformal Education	Informal Education
Structured Systemic Institutionalized	Nonsystemic Organized activity	Based on life and experience

of flexibility in relation to sponsorship and control, curricula, participants, goals, and the evaluation of outcomes.[5]

These distinctions serve to indicate the nature of the relationship between the education experienced by participants and the existing social and educational structures. In formal education the relationship or proximity is close between participants and established educational structures. This is the case because those persons with authority control the educational experience. Within a formal system the potential for an emphasis upon conformity to institutionalized norms and expectations is high. But formal education may also afford the greatest possible distance from societal or communal structures and norms if the ethos of the institution is intentionally critical and distinct from prevailing structures and norms in the wider society. Such a situation assumes that the school has the freedom to maintain a distinct countercultural perspective in relation to other social structures.

Both social and educational structures vary in the extent to which they allow for flexibility and deviance from stated or accepted norms. Informal education affords the greatest potential for individualized or unconstrained educational experience because of its potential distance from formal institutional norms; but informal education may also promote closer conformity to prevailing

5. Thomas J. La Belle provides a discussion of these distinctions in *Nonformal Education in Latin America and the Caribbean: Stability, Reform and Revolution* (New York: Praeger, 1986), 1–10. See also P. Coombs and M. Ahmed, *Attacking Rural Poverty: How Nonformal Education Can Help* (Baltimore: Johns Hopkins University Press, 1974).

societal and communal structures and norms, for toleration of deviance or nonconformity varies in different settings. For example, a particular congregation may enforce conformity to existing norms to such an extent that persons receive support only for knowledge, skills, and insights that enhance but never question the life of that community. Participants within a formal educational setting may also be instructed in the hidden curriculum but not encouraged or allowed to consider alternative life or world views. One may question whether education is being provided for students in either of these settings or whether the experiences should be described as indoctrination or conditioning, with either thought or behavior prescribed for participants. The terms *indoctrination* and *conditioning* tend to have negative connotations in a society that views any imposition upon individuals or individuality as inappropriate and restrictive of human freedom. But we must recognize that education does address the thought and behavior of participants and does seek to influence persons without manipulating them. Thus educators confront a dilemma: How can they most effectively share the accumulated wisdom of the ages with participants in formal and nonformal education and still allow for the expression of human freedom and creativity? How can educators provide a necessary structure and yet allow discovery and creativity? This question raises the perennial issue of how to balance freedom and form in social life.[6]

6. John H. Westerhoff III ("The Making of Christians Through Formation," unpublished article, Duke University Divinity School, Durham, N.C., 1990) describes three processes in relation to this dilemma, which he distinguishes as formation, instruction, and education. Instruction and formation could be equated with the emphasis upon conformity and the continuity of a tradition and norm or the provision of a necessary structure. Instruction can be viewed as a positive process as compared with indoctrination, but both focus upon the thoughts of participants. Formation can be viewed as a positive process as compared with conditioning, but both focus upon the behavior of participants. The third process, education, enables students to explore alternatives and imagine new structures and norms beyond those honored and fostered by a particular social or educational structure. Westerhoff's perspective affirms the need for structure in life and the corresponding need for norms. Along with other Christian and religious educators in the United States, Westerhoff emphasizes the formation of persons as the key process for bringing about renewal in Christian education. A similar stance is taken by the evangelical educator Lawrence Richards and by C. Ellis Nelson in the mainline Protestant tradition.

64

It is important to consider how formal, nonformal, and informal education relate to the educational trinity of content, persons, and the context of community and society (chap. 1). Formal education emphasizes content and its systematic instruction through schooling. Nonformal education focuses on the community or society, especially the socialization and formation of members or participants of that community or society. Informal education emphasizes persons and the daily, routine experiences that provide the occasions for discovery and self-education. A definition of education that incorporates the systematic instruction of formal education, the socialization and formation of nonformal education, and the self-education of informal education is proposed by Cremin. He defined education as "the deliberate, systematic, and sustained effort to transmit, evoke, or acquire knowledge, attitudes, values, skills, or sensibilities, as well as any outcomes of that effort."[7] Such a broad understanding of education helps us in exploring the impact of continuing and changing educational structures.

Continuing and Changing Structures

In order to assess the impact of social and educational structures in the Christian education of persons across the life span, one must consider the educative role of the family, the community, the economy, agencies, the church, the media, the school, and the body politic. All of these structures are charac-

---

One concern that must be raised in relation to the emphasis upon formation is the extent to which a particular community or society can be viewed as faithful and therefore worthy of serving as a model or an example for the next generation. Such a commitment to formation may limit the predisposition of faith communities faced with new challenges to hear the prophetic voice that calls for repentance, an alternative way of life, and faithfulness to the Christian vocation. Nevertheless, to expand upon an understanding of education beyond schooling and formal education, Christian educators must consider the impact of families, communities, economies, social and voluntary agencies, churches, the media, and political bodies. In addition, they must assess the impact of various schools.

7. Cremin, *Traditions of American Education*. 134. For a discussion of Cremin's definition see Robert W. Pazmiño, *Foundational Issues in Christian Education: An Introduction in Evangelical Perspective* (Grand Rapids: Baker, 1988), 75–80.

terized both by continuity and by change, with patterns of influence rooted in the past. Also, the educative role of each structure will vary in different contexts and with individuals; exceptions can be cited for the general observations made here. While this variability presents a unique challenge to the educator, it also fosters an appreciation of the rich diversity of humankind. Such diversity can be celebrated and appreciated in the human community even as we recognize the need for unity and commonality in the formation of communities.

The Family

Given the numerous changes that have affected the understanding of family life in the United States since the 1960s, the initial issue to explore is the definition of family itself. The divorce rate has increased, the number of women in the work force has risen, single-parent homes and blended or reconstituted families have become commonplace, and increasing pressures on the traditional family structure have caused some to evaluate the family in new ways. The affirmation of single adults and their lifestyle has also raised the question of how families are defined and constituted. The experience of women in Latin America who have suffered the disappearance of husbands and children also poses a challenge to whether the use of the term *family* itself can adequately incorporate them without perpetuating their suffering. One definition that has been proposed to embrace this diversity of experience is that a family consists of persons living in a common household or related through a biological network. This definition includes the nuclear, extended, and single-parent families or households, but it allows for the reduction of the notion of a family to that of a household. It is possible to distinguish a family from a household, with a household being a spatial term referring to the dwelling places or the physical belongings of people with a stress upon economic and political relationships. By contrast, an understanding of family would stress the kinship and relational dimensions of life in which people and their values are of primary concern, rather than spatial or physical qualities.[8]

8. See Charles R. Foster, "The Changing Family," in *Religious Education as Social Transformation,* ed. Allen J. Moore (Birmingham, Ala.: Religious Education Press, 1989), 50–57.

Another definition is one that was proposed in the Vatican II documents, which describe the family as the "first and vital cell of society."[9] This definition denotes the importance and the inclusion of all persons in that cell, and it recognizes the cell as a social structure, but it does not help in discerning the nature or quality of that cell.

Samuel M. Natale has provided yet a third definition, which views the family as a system of interdependent relationships, engaged in change and adaptation, and geared to the growth and support of each member.[10] Natale's definition assumes that the family is functional, at least in its intent. But the increased awareness of dysfunctional families points up the realities with which persons must contend in family systems that do not provide support for their members. Nevertheless, even members of dysfunctional families intend to provide growth and support in their relationships, and thus they can be called families.

Gloria Durka provides additional insights as she defines a family as a group of persons who consider themselves bound to each other by enduring ties and responsible for each other's well-being.[11] Family life education from this perspective is the effort to promote the development of the family as a functional system for the mutual support of its members and, if the meaning of "well-being" includes social realities, which it must, to promote their vocations in the community, society, and world. With this expansion, Durka's definition provides a feasible way to understand the family, even in the case of a dysfunctional family, which can be encouraged to be increasingly functional.

Once the question of defining family is considered, a second question must be raised in relation to the educative role of the family. In recounting the educational history of the United States, Cremin observed: "The education of the home is often decisive and educative styles first learned in the family hold much of the key to the patterns by which individuals

9. *Apostolicam Actuositatem* (Decree on the Apostolate of the Laity), *The Documents of Vatican II*, 11.

10. Samuel M. Natale, "A Family Systems Approach to Religious Education and Development," *Religious Education* 74 (May–June 1979): 247.

11. Gloria Durka, "Family Life Education," in *Harper's Encyclopedia of Religious Education*, ed. Iris V. Cully and Kendig B. Cully (San Francisco: Harper and Row, 1990), 254.

engage in, move through, and combine educational experiences over a lifetime."[12] Exceptions to this general observation can be cited, but the implication for the discussion of educational structures is clear. Serious attention must be given to the place the family has in the education of persons, and the Christian church must support families in their efforts to be positive educational influences in the lives of their members. The family has also been described as a mediating structure in society that provides an interface between individuals and the wider community and society. This description appropriately focuses on the key communal and public role that the family can play, versus a view of the family that stresses only individual gratification or protection.

Such a concern for the family must not be interpreted to exclude the significant place of single adults and the variety of forms in which families are organized in society. Jesus himself was a single adult, and any "family-focused" program must be challenged as to whether Jesus, if present in our time, would be a welcomed participant. In cultures outside of the dominant Anglo orientation of North America, the ethos of family can embrace a wide variety of persons and might be more appropriately described as a household or micro-community that affirms the extended and inclusive family. The common human experience and need identified in the naming of family are affiliation and intimacy where individuals can be supported and loved while being needed by and supportive of others. Family is also a setting in which persons can risk vulnerability and honestly disclose their feelings and thoughts to others who make some effort to understand and empathize. Such expectations for the family result in the inevitable evaluation of some aspects of family life as dysfunctional, given the realities of human sin in both communal and personal realms. Certainly the Christian faith, which upholds the place of forgiveness, healing, and reconciliation, offers these as choices to the dysfunctional family. But with the rise of abuse and irreconcilable situations, other considerations must also be named where the continued survival and health of family members are at risk in some existing families. The most difficult decision I had to make while

12. Cremin, *Traditions of American Education*, 122.

working as a crisis counselor in a day hospital program for emotionally disturbed children was to advocate the removal of a child from a home with his grandparents, his only surviving family members, because of their dysfunctional relationships. This decision required court action and public recognition that this family was unfit to provide the care and nurture needed by a child.

In relation to the structure of the family, one must assess the extent to which any particular family allows for individualization without succumbing to the individualism of North American society that does not foster a sense of the commonweal. A functional family structure may so stress conformity and continuity with traditions and expectations that persons may not be able effectively to explore their personal or public identity. One's judgment of the health of a family depends a great deal upon one's definition of health or functionality, and that definition is highly influenced by cultural norms. One must question the assumption that a single-adult, female-headed household is dysfunctional.

Durka's definition of family considers being bound to one another by enduring ties and of being responsible for each other's well-being. A norm that has been historically associated with well-being in the United States is the possibility of individualization in which persons can affirm their autonomy while recognizing an enduring interdependence. But various cultures define the place of autonomy and interdependence differently and make gender distinctions in relation to such norms. The pluralistic and multicultural realities in the United States require careful description and the recognition and affirmation of differences in relation to one's understanding of autonomy and interdependence. Historically, autonomy has been associated with the orientation of males, and the importance of relationships has been associated with females. But persons of both sexes need opportunities for relationships and spaces where autonomy can be exercised.

The family includes not only parent(s) who serve as the primary educators, but also siblings and extended or adopted family members. The term *adopted* here refers to those who function as significant others and role models for children and youths within the family system. As a parent with children in elementary school and college, I can appreciate the role that grandparents can play in the life of both children and youth. In addition to those associated through blood relations, people bonded to a family unit can have a significant and formative influence. This also suggests that the family can enable its members to function effectively in the wider community and society. Charles Foster observes that "the nature of the family is relational—between man and woman, between parents and children, across successive generations, and among siblings."[13]

With such a relational nature the family can embrace a connective and linking function, which it can have between its members and the other structures and agencies of society. The family can foster the web of life across religious, economic, political, educational, social, and cultural structures. In addition, the family itself may assume some of these other functions, which, though associated with earlier historical arrangements and disassociated from modern industrialized social structures, enable persons to discern the wholeness of life. This has been the case for a number of ethnic and cultural groups in the United States. But in so doing, the family can honor and embody traditions and values distinct from the wider social realities and provide a place where excluded knowledge can be named. In this way the family serves a mediating role to help individuals gain perspective and a healthy distance from those currents in the community and society that may not support the well-being of family members. One example of such a positive influence of the family is when a neighborhood drug culture is countered by strong models and encouragement to seek values and lifestyles alternative to those proposed in the wider community or by peers.

The Community

As was the case in exploring the family, one encounters the immediate need to define community in order to discuss its importance as an educational structure. A community can be defined as a group of persons who affirm and maintain a common unity of purpose and action in the world over time. This

13. Foster, "The Changing Family," 58.

unity is often expressed in terms of shared memory, vision, mission, authority, rituals, and relationships that serve to provide the vital connection or linkage among persons.[14] For a community to be perpetuated, procedures develop to initiate and to support persons in the common heritage, which itself may be undergoing change. A community develops its distinct world view and ethos, which distinguishes its character or culture from other communities. Education in the community can then be viewed as the passing of this culture from one generation to the next generations.[15]

What has been described up to this point may lead one to view a community only in terms of continuity. But communities also embrace elements of discontinuity and change where inherited patterns are renewed and transformed. This renewal and transformation result in a living tradition and a culture that is open to appropriate change as a community interacts with its ever-changing context. In defining its identity each community explicitly or implicitly names those aspects of its heritage that are negotiable and subject to change and those aspects that are nonnegotiable and to be preserved. By naming the nonnegotiables, a community establishes its own boundaries and distinctives, but may also encounter other boundaries that are imposed by other communities and the larger society.

Boundaries between communities hold the potential both to define and to divide persons. The wisdom often quoted in relation to this challenge of negotiating boundaries is to have unity in the essentials, diversity in the nonessentials, but love in all things. A tension often develops at the point of naming the essentials, which can vary greatly for different members of the same community. Drawing upon the insights of Talcott Parsons, Donald E. Miller suggests that a community has a number of dynamic elements, which include interacting individuals, normative practices, symbolized meanings, and a shared envi-

14. John H. Westerhoff III, "Framing an Alternative for the Future of Catechesis," in *A Faithful Church: Issues in the History of Catechesis*, ed. John H. Westerhoff III and O. C. Edwards, Jr. (Wilton, Conn.: Morehouse-Barlow, 1981), 302.

15. Bailyn defines education as "the entire process by which a culture transmits itself across the generations." See *Education in the Forming of American Society*, 14.

71

ronment. He then defines a community as a group of persons sharing common commitments, norms of behavior, symbolic culture, and living within a shared environment. Shared commitments refers to individual loyalty to the community; shared norms, to both formal institutions and customary practices; and shared symbols, to language, thought, and the whole range of cultural expression. The shared environment is the place of residence and activity, the nexus of causes that condition the common life, and the various conditions that shape patterns of interaction. All of these elements are present when a group is a community in the fullest sense.[16]

Using Miller's definition of community, educators need to focus on the processes whereby the commitments, norms, culture, and environment are communicated to or shared with prospective and current members of the community. These processes include formal, nonformal, and informal education. The act of sharing a common life together promotes informal education. But for a community to be sustained over time some explicit formal education or implicit nonformal education is often needed. Each community is presented with the challenge that it is one generation away from extinction. Such a challenge requires some mechanisms to insure the continuing life of the community.

Westerhoff has named several elements that ensure the continued life of communities and, in particular, communities of faith. These elements are a common memory or story; a common vision of goals and means for life together; a common authority for resolving conflicts; and a shared life that includes a common mission, relationships, and rituals.[17] Communities must devise means by which people can participate in and own their distinctives but perhaps transform them in the process of appropriation. Each community will identify which aspects of these elements are essential and not subject to change or nego-

16. Donald E. Miller, *Story and Context: An Introduction to Christian Education* (Nashville: Abingdon, 1987), 18. Miller makes use of the faith community model of Christian education in his work and thus follows in the tradition of Horace Bushnell. C. Ellis Nelson and Lawrence O. Richards are other Christian educators who use the community or socialization model to develop their understanding of education. For their earlier works see C. Ellis Nelson, *Where Faith Begins* (Atlanta: John Knox, 1971); and Richards, *Christian Education*.
17. Westerhoff, in *A Faithful Church*, 302.

72

tiation, and which aspects are nonessential and subject to change and negotiation. Identifying and sanctioning these aspects raises the real possibility of conflict along with the celebration of points of continuity in the life of a community. The task of educators or teachers in the community is to share perspectives and to raise questions concerning these elements. Educators can thus serve as both a conserving and subversive presence in the community.[18] When the subversive or prophetic role challenges a community to confront areas that need confession and change, educators take a risk by assuming that role.

In describing the nature of Christian community, some scholars have proposed that a family might best portray the distinctives affirmed by the Christian faith for guiding relationships. The image of a household or a family of faith might well support positive associations for persons who have experienced healthy relationships in their family of origin, but a number of individuals find such an image inappropriate or not fitting. In Latin America those whose loved ones have disappeared also find that emphasis upon a family image does not inspire the formation of community. Thus the image that best describes koinonia might be an inclusive one that embraces people who are single, married, divorced, or remarried, with various experiences in their families of origin. All of these persons are invited to participate in a community of faith that finds its unity in the person and work of Jesus Christ, who himself was a single person. Such a community incorporates forgiven sinners into a corporate relationship with one another and the triune God. The trinity, which incorporates three persons into a cosmic unity, can serve as a model for the human community. The challenge for the human community is to reflect the unity and life that are experienced in almighty God who creates, redeems, and sustains.

The Economy

Naming the economy might appear unusual in considering educational structures. Nevertheless, with some thought it is

18. For a comparison of the subversive and conserving aspects of education see Neil Postman and Charles Weingartner, *Teaching as Subversive Activity* (New York: Delacorte, 1969); and Neil Postman, *Teaching as Conserving Activity* (New York: Dell, 1980).

possible to identify the important linkages that exist between education and the economy in a particular society. For instance, a student of educational history might be surprised to find that during the colonial period in the United States, the household itself played a crucial role in educating persons for a place in the economy. One would typically be trained to assume the occupation of one's parents or one was apprenticed to others to learn a trade or a craft. In the case of women, training in the various tasks required to maintain and support a household was provided by one's mother or other women in the home. This education for a productive position or place in the community was seen as a major responsibility and was crucial for survival. Bernard Bailyn, an educational historian who described the role of education in the United States in colonial times, names the economy as one of the four axles of society (the others were the family, the community, and the church.)[19]

If one recognizes the importance of work in all areas of human endeavor, then the place of learning and training for participation in the workplace becomes a matter of concern. The structures of schooling itself can be viewed as one means by which persons are prepared for being productive in a chosen occupation or profession. Some of the lessons taught in a schooling setting may be transferred to the workplace: the need to respect authority, to be on time, to complete one's assignments efficiently and correctly, to work competitively and/or cooperatively, and to accept the feedback or compensation provided by one's teacher or employer. These lessons may not be perfectly learned and exceptions exist, but generally the expectation in business is that schooling will prepare persons for entry into the job market. An issue of greater concern is how persons view their work and gain fulfillment from active participation in their work, chosen or assigned.

Questions of one's attitudes toward work and the values perceived in one's work bring under consideration societal and cultural factors. Questions of the ownership of the means of production and benefits from the fruits of production have been debated by capitalists and socialists. But a question posed by the Christian faith has been the place of human vocation and

19. Bailyn, *Education in the Forming of American Society*, 45.

the use of one's gifts, talents, and energies for the service of God and the benefit of the community and society. Often this question is secondary in contexts where the need for survival is primary, extensive unemployment is an issue, and the right to work is at stake. Paul G. Johnson, a Lutheran clergyman, has convincingly proposed that grace be considered as God's work ethic, with the need to make explicit the connections between the gospel and weekday work.[20] The value of individuals must not be equated with societally sanctioned productive work, which poses a particular challenge for those who are not employed in society or are retired from gainful employment. Gabriel Moran helpfully suggests that work is the aim of all education, provided that work is defined to include play, art, and the tasks associated with women's work such as birthing, feeding, clothing, cleaning, healing, burying, and in general, child care.[21] This broadened understanding of work as the expression of care for the world and others suggests that education needs to foster the development of persons in giving care.

Social Agencies

Beyond the influence of the family, the community, and the economy, a host of social agencies and groups engage in the education and formation of persons. In my experience, the Cub Scouts, Boy Scouts, and Explorers provided nonformal education that supported and complemented the messages of the family, the local church and community, and the public school in relation to values and the nature of social life. These scouting groups all held their meetings in the church my family and I attended through my childhood and youth. My father, who was a deacon in the church, also served as the institutional representative from the church to the local scouting board. Thus these voluntary associations provided a significant influence, which in my personal experience served to confirm and complement the instruction provided by my family, church, and community.

20. Paul G. Johnson, *Grace: God's Work Ethic, Making Connections Between the Gospel and Weekday Work* (Valley Forge, Penn.: Judson, 1985).

21. Gabriel Moran, *Religious Education Development: Images for the Future* (Minneapolis: Winston, 1983), 171–72.

Another cluster of agencies formative in my educational history included the network of public libraries and museums in Brooklyn, New York. I made regular visits to these agencies not only to complete school assignments, but also to explore areas of personal interest. During one year in junior high school a good friend and I made weekly subway trips to the Brooklyn Museum to pick up slides for a social studies class that was studying ancient Greece and Rome. These regular trips provided occasions to explore all the niches of the museum and the adjoining Brooklyn Botanical Gardens. Such exposure added a dimension to our education not possible in the classroom and encouraged a process of exploration and discovery. What has not been mentioned up to this point is the role of self-direction and self-education that in part determines how any individual will interact with the educational structures already identified. The effects of any of the structures are influenced by the unique learning style of each person.

In addition to the local, state, and federal agencies in the United States, parachurch agencies also need to be mentioned. These agencies represent a variety of independent, interdependent, and dependent relationships with church and denominational structures, and have close or loose ties with churches. The agencies provide an array of programs for children, youth, and adults, along with opportunities for intergenerational interactions. A particular challenge in relation to social agencies is the need for coordinating their influences in the life of children and youth.

The Church

In a text addressing Christian education one would be remiss to ignore the church as an educational structure. This focus on structure does not limit considering the church as a people of God who are gathered and scattered in different settings. But it does suggest that the relationships and interactions in the life of the church can be viewed as a structure or system that in and of itself communicates certain ways of life. Such ways of life include choices about knowledge, values, and attitudes considered worth passing on to others and being embodied in the life of the faith community itself. For example, one value maintained relative to church membership might be to include everyone. This value would seem to follow from a commitment to express love to all participants in the life of the community. But this value may be in conflict with the need to maintain a clear sense of identity in a community identified as "Christian." In being Christian, the community may need to exclude individuals from formal membership, though not from participation, who do not identify themselves as followers of Jesus Christ. Thus for any community there is a need to define and maintain boundaries that provide a sense of identity. Some may interpret this stance as an appropriate commitment to the truth of the gospel, which calls for identification with the person and work of Jesus Christ; others may see it as a narrow and exclusive position that does not allow for religious plurality in an age of inclusivity.

One issue of particular concern in churches in the United States is the relationship between clergy and laity. A traditional structure in the church may maintain clearly differentiated roles between the clergy and laity, with the clergy providing leadership and the laity providing "followership" for the proper functioning of the church system. Such a traditional structure has been questioned historically with the Reformation affirmation of the priesthood and prophethood of all believers, and the recent affirmation of the ministry of all believers. Such a shift requires the establishment of norms to guide the relationship of laity and clergy in a way that recognizes the proper exercise of authority, giftedness, and leadership. Gabriel Fackre, a Congregational systematic theologian, has suggested that clergy have ministries of identity, whereas laity have ministries of vitality. By this he does not mean that clergy cannot be vital in faith or that laity cannot be identified with the faith, but that a functional division, a division in office, exists. Such a functional division serves to identify priorities of focus in ministry. Fackre also indicates the wider context of ministry that emphasizes mutuality, partnership, and interdependence between laity and clergy in their diverse ministries.[22]

22. Gabriel Fackre, "Christ's Ministry and Ours," in *The Laity in Ministry: The Whole People of God for the Whole World,* ed. George Peck and John S. Hoffman (Valley Forge, Penn.: Judson, 1984), 111–15.

In addition to the nature of relationships between laity and clergy within the church, the nature of relationships between children, youth, and adults must be considered. If Christian education seeks to enable the adults of the faith community to pass on the faith to the next generations, then the place of children and youth must be examined. One issue of particular volatility in some congregations is whether to have children present during the worship service or to maintain a separate worship experience for children, appropriate for their developmental needs. The question then is whether the worship service is viewed primarily as an adult-centered experience. If worship is intended to be an intergenerational experience where persons of all ages can attend and participate at their own level of ability, then the absence of children and youth poses a problem.[23]

In a number of congregations in New England the practice is to hold an educational hour at the same time as the worship service. This arrangement structurally separates worship as an adult experience from education as an experience for children and youth along with those adults who are serving as teachers. A separate educational hour is not provided for adults, with church participation limited to one hour on Sunday mornings. In this structure adults generally do not sense the need to be involved in Christian education, and children and youth do not value the experience of corporate worship on Sunday morning.[24] Children often have not actively participated in worship and have not had an opportunity to see and learn from adults as they participate in worship. Then when youth and young adults elect not to attend church, resulting in a significant drop in participation, church leaders are in a quandary regarding the reasons for the decline. In addition, adults who volunteer to teach often attribute their lack of spiritual nourishment to time spent teaching without the opportunity to worship regularly with the congregation. Within such a structure the recruitment of teach-

23. For a good introductory work to intergenerational Christian education see James W. White, *Intergenerational Religious Education* (Birmingham, Ala.: Religious Education Press, 1988).

24. The impact of this structure can be referred to as the "null curriculum" (see chap. 4).

ers is a constant problem, and many adults agree to serve only for a very short term, which limits the consistency of relationships with children and youth that is required for effective modeling and Christian education.

Some people think of the influence of the church in education only in terms of the church school or the Sunday school. This emphasis supports a definition of education that stresses formal education or schooling to the relative exclusion of nonformal and informal education. However, nonformal education occurs in the church through group and committee meetings and any regular events that include some aspects of teaching. Informal education occurs through the opportunities that the church community has to gather and share its common life. This education includes such events as church suppers, picnics, retreats, outings, and worship services, which all embody what the faith community honors, values, and seeks to pass on to newcomers, strangers, and the succeeding generations. Some educators advocate the need for church education to move away from a schooling model and to embrace a socialization or an enculturation model for its most effective teaching efforts. Advocates of this approach include C. Ellis Nelson, John Westerhoff, and Larry Richards. The strength of their position comes from recognizing the distinctive contributions that church life can make to individuals in the formation of their faith as it is vitally connected with life. This type of formation is best realized as the church functions as a strong community that supports and nurtures a wide of variety of persons across the life span.

The Media

The media exert a major educational influence in modern industrialized society with a vast communication structure that supports its production and consumption worldwide. Media include television, radio, cinema, the press (which produces newspapers and periodicals), and a host of new and developing multimedia technologies that include the audio and video recording and computer industries. For many young persons in the West, the media, in particular television, have become the major educational agents that promote what is true, real, good, valuable, and worthy in life. Commentators on popular trends in the United States have identified a shift from an emphasis on print to one on images and sound bites. With this shift a number of adjustments must be made to provide people with the critical skills needed not only to interpret the unending barrage of messages and images, but also to respond faithfully and creatively. A key question to be considered by Christians is the extent to which the church must accommodate this media revolution and the extent to which alternatives or countercultural approaches must be maintained. For example, should church school curricula make extensive use of the new media at increased costs or should personal relationships and systematically reasoned approaches be stressed to complement the media diet? Perhaps both options should be pursued, but on what terms?

One must recognize the tremendous effect television has had since the 1950s in considering education at the end of the twentieth century. The effect has both positive and negative dimensions. The positive influences, both actual and potential, have been educational, recreational, cultural, and religious. Educationally, information on global events and realities has been made accessible to more people, and, in some cases, this exposure has stimulated reading and study along with acquisition of a common culture. Some programming, such as public television's "Sesame Street," has helped children with basic skills. Television has also provided entertainment and diversion for the public. Through primarily public, but also commercial television, cultural, social, and political events have been available for general viewing. Of some significance for the religious community has been the provision of another vehicle for sharing its perspectives and distinctives through preaching and teaching, especially for those who cannot attend public events. These positive results must be compared with the negative aspects of television.

Four major negative possibilities can be named, with corresponding consequences especially upon children. First, television can take the place of normal play or recreational activity. Second, television has been an effective teacher in providing multiple stimuli through sounds, visual images, and games, with the result that traditional learning is less stimulating and less valued. Third, television provides the illusion of friendship and has served as an electronic babysitter that never punishes, disciplines, or corrects. Fourth, children become part of the television experience and identify with the characters portrayed on the screen.[25]

Children may develop a sense of spectatorship about life that encourages passivity. They can also develop a false concept of realities, such as the family always being happy and able to resolve conflicts in a thirty- to sixty-minute format. Television portrayals of violence, sex, stereotyping, and materialism distort the realities of life for children. Television's time distortions can discourage patience in learning tasks. The school performance of children has been affected through excessive viewing of a primary diet of adult programming. The values promoted through commercial programming can often be in conflict with those embraced by a Christian family, church, and community. Television viewing has also been implicated in the squelching of children's imagination and in the disintegration of family meal time.[26]

All such results are not exclusively caused by television, but work in concert with other factors operating in society. With such a potential catalogue of negative effects, one can appreciate the arguments of Jerry Mander for the elimination of television.[27] But one must at least be aware of the need to control children's viewing and to educate those who care for children regarding these potential negative forces. Ignoring such ten-

25. Nancy Jessen (seminar on television viewing, Beverly, Mass., 13 February 1984) has named these impacts from her elementary school experience and specialization in learning disabilities. For additional sources that discuss the impact of television see the following: Annenberg School of Communication, University of Pennsylvania and the Gallup Organization, Inc., *Religion and Television* (Philadelphia: Annenberg School of Communication, University of Pennsylvania, 1984); George Comstock et al., *Television and Human Behavior* (New York: Columbia University Press, 1978); Neil Postman, *Amusing Ourselves to Death: Public Discourse in the Age of Show Business* (New York: Viking, 1985); and Neil Postman, *The Disappearance of Childhood* (New York: Delacorte, 1982).

26. Jessen, seminar on television viewing.

27. Jerry Mander, *Four Arguments for the Elimination of Television* (New York: Morrow Quill Paperbacks, 1978).

dencies limits the educational heritage for present and future generations. Advocating the constructive use and development of the media is a needed priority in a culture increasingly dominated by the media.

The School

The school represents the one educational structure most commonly associated with education in the United States and in many countries worldwide. In this context one must consider the school system, which encompasses a complex bureaucratic structure of persons and programs that seek to meet the educational needs of a given community, town, city, state, or nation. But for those parents who have school-age children the first association centers on local public, private, parochial, or home schools.

A number of schooling choices are available to some persons but not others in the United States, so we must consider six factors that influence the choice of schooling. These include availability, marks of quality, beliefs and convictions, resources, student needs, and parental experiences. Other factors can be named, but these serve to identify the nature of the interaction between schooling structures and the parents or guardians who explicitly or implicitly support these structures in varying degrees by having their children participate.[28]

The first factor is the available options that parents and their children may have in any given community. Stephen Arons, in evaluating the current schooling options in the United States, observed that there is "freedom of choice for the wealthy, compulsory education for the rest."[29] An exception to Arons's observation would hold for students who apply to well-endowed schools that have blind admission policies for financial need or for exceptional students whose education is mandated by the

28. For a helpful summary of research findings that can assist in the consideration of schools, see *What Works: Research About Teaching and Learning* (Washington, D.C.: United States Department of Education, 1986), 44–62; and R. Kyle, ed., *Reaching for Excellence: An Effective Schools Sourcebook* (Washington, D.C.: U.S. Government Printing Office, 1985).

29. Stephen Arons, "Educational Choice as a Civil Rights Strategy," in *Public Values: Private Schools*, ed. Neal E. Evans (Philadelphia: Falmer, 1989), 74.

law. Such policies and laws can address the impact of classism and increase the diversity among students in a school. One must also recognize the legal constraint that requires children and youth of a particular age to be in attendance at some school. For many this limits options to the public schools in a given community. For others, options may include parochial or private schools, assuming that financial resources are available. These resources may be accessible through family, community, outside funding sources, or through a school itself. A perennial question to raise in relation to availability is the equity of access to schooling options.

A second factor is the quality of the schooling. My two children have had schooling experiences in a variety of settings and arrangements, and I can name thirteen marks of quality that can be used to assess a school:

1. A clear statement and understanding of a philosophy or a vision of education that guides the work of the school.
2. Competent administrators who coordinate the educational program with and through people. Effective administrators can use the existing organization and work for change where it is needed.
3. The presence of competent teachers and support personnel. Teachers are the backbone of a school; capable teachers create an environment in which students can learn.
4. The curriculum itself, which should provide basic academic preparation, address exceptional needs, and allow for creativity and individuality in learning.
5. The possibility of extracurricular activities that can serve to help develop whole persons and foster integration between the classroom and life.
6. Diversity among staff and students along with a sense of unity amidst that diversity. Some may prefer homogeneity to diversity, but such a stance is difficult to defend in our multicultural, multiracial, and pluralistic world.
7. The nature of peer relations in the school, because persons can learn a great deal from their peers. One gauge

of peer relations is the extent to which members of the school develop friendships and a sense of community and loyalty.

8. The nature of parental involvements in elementary and secondary schools. In adult and higher education this mark relates to the involvements of one's immediate or extended family in the life of the school.

9. The size of the school, the faculty-student ratio, and other demographic factors such as the faculty and staff turnover. Bigger is not always better if the quality of relationships is valued in the school community. It is difficult to maintain a sense of community with large numbers of people who cannot be named or recognized.

10. For Christians and for other religious groups, the school's openness to a religious world view. Some Christians prefer a narrowly defined and subscribed world view, whereas others prefer a broader, inclusive world view. These world views might be roughly equated with conservative, liberal, and radical theological and ideological stances, but not exclusively so.

11. The quality of the facilities in which the education is provided. But one must recognize that excellent education can occur in the most limited of facilities.

12. The sensitivity of the school to the continuity and change of the cultural capital or content. I refer to the need to maintain essentials such as reading, writing, and arithmetic while providing exposure to new developments in knowledge such as computer competencies. These essentials are to be taught along with creative arts and expression.

13. The track record of the school, its successes and failures in the past, and its efforts to build upon the successes and address the failures. Sensitivity to the past is important in being faithful to one's mission in the present and future.

In addition to the second factor, quality, a third factor that can influence the choice of schooling is the nature of parental and community beliefs and convictions regarding schooling itself. Different families and communities view their responsibilities for educating their members from distinct perspectives. The majority of families and communities, including church communities, expect schools to confirm or complement their efforts to pass on their heritage and to form persons. But in a pluralistic society areas of conflict often emerge between the expectations, beliefs, and convictions of a particular family or religious community and the school. Political and social realities often require compromise in addressing these conflicts, but certain groups will not opt to compromise and will instead seek alternative educational experiences for their members.

A fourth factor is the availability of resources, both human and material, for the type of schooling selected. The costs of education must be considered in terms of time, energies, commitments, and finances. During doctoral studies and with a limited income, my family had to make sacrifices to send a child to parochial and then private school because of the conditions in the local public school. In the case of home schooling, which is gaining in popularity, key factors are the parents' abilities and availability. Parents' competencies to teach may not be adequate and may need to be supplemented. But every parent is involved in home schooling in a general sense, no matter what formal schooling option is selected. While serving as a house husband during years of graduate study, I often spent one to two hours each day supplementing a child's schooling experiences, providing individual attention that was not possible in classroom settings.

Student needs are a fifth major factor influencing the choice of a school. The individual needs of children, youth, and adults can vary greatly. The author's son always needed an intellectual challenge. That eventually led him to consider boarding schools for secondary education. Public schools are committed to meet the educational needs of a wide variety of students, but in some communities alternatives must be actively sought. I discovered that even with very limited resources, some alternatives were to be found. Others may not be as fortunate or blessed.

A sixth and final factor is parental experience. Positive experiences can foster the valuing of a particular schooling option for one's child, or a negative experience can result in the active exploration of alternatives to those a parent encountered. This assumes that options are in fact viable. In my family, one child has explored an educational pilgrimage different from those of both parents in primary and secondary education, with attendance at public, private, and parochial schools. The primary-school experience of the second child has been similar to those of the parents, but the exposure to preschool education and kindergarten in a private school abroad was not shared by either parent.

The Body Politic

In considering educational structures, one must not ignore the effect that political bodies have upon education. From the approach of Aristotle, politics can be defined as the art of making and keeping persons truly human.[30] The challenge posed in using this definition is the description of true humanity. A Christian can say that God is involved in politics through the reign of Jesus Christ. Through their faith people can become more fully human and can enhance the humanity of others through their diverse ministries in the world. True humanity is thus described from this perspective in relation to the person of Jesus of Nazareth. One could then identify the politics of God or the politics of Jesus in relation to the values of love, faith, hope, truth, righteousness, justice, and peace in life and in education. These are the values of the reign or kingdom of God of which Jesus spoke in his earthly ministry. But in relation to earthly body politic or political bodies it is possible to see how political realities and decisions affect education. This can be seen in the aims of education, the nature of the relationships fostered in schools, the availability of human and material resources, the access to educational opportunities, and the power of persons to make decisions in these and other areas.

30. George W. Webber, *The Congregation in Mission* (New York: Abingdon, 1964), 49. In this definition Webber draws upon the work of Paul Lehmann, *Ethics in a Christian Context* (New York: Harper and Row, 1963), 74–101.

The aims of education are influenced by various political bodies, and political and economic factors influence those who make educational decisions. In a democratic and capitalist political system one aim implicit in education is to foster the formation of active citizens who can be productive workers and consumers. In a democratic and socialist political system one aim implicit in education is to foster the formation of active citizens who can work cooperatively and hold the corporate good over individual good. These aims or goals may not actually be reached in the case of every student, but they set the parameters under which education is practiced and set the tradition or norm that is embraced, changed, or rejected in the case of individual schools or persons.

Political structures also affect the nature of relationships fostered in the schools and other educational programs. In general, a hierarchical pattern maintains that students are subject to teachers, teachers are subject to administrators, and administrators are subject to school board members. Such a pattern reflects the nature of relationships that exist in the economic structures of society with employees being subject to supervisors, supervisors subject to employers, and employers subject to board members. This simple structure may be amplified to include cooperative and collaborative groupings and the possibility of representative and participatory engagement, but the basic pattern persists. In the United States the school's pattern is further complicated by the role of parents and communities in local control of education.

A third impact of political structures is in the area of the availability of human and material resources for education. Political bodies in many communities provide the financial resources needed to fund public schooling efforts and in some cases provide resources for private education. Through their certification and licensing powers these bodies also control access to teaching and administrative positions. In a time of limited resources, political decisions have a major effect upon which programs are sustained and which are not. Difficult choices must be made and the question of priorities is an essential one both before and during crises.

87

Access to educational opportunities is a fourth area in which political structures function. Equity of access to the educational capital, especially at the college and graduate level, that any particular society possesses raises recurrent questions, and the existence of higher education assumes that an elite has access to resources that are not available to the entire population. Even with the popularization of education in the United States, some persons cannot afford to attend. Thus, decisions made by those with political power influence the demographics of future leaders in society, especially in those areas where education is an increasingly important qualification. Claims that a meritocracy (i.e., those who have merit are provided with access to higher education) exists within a democracy must be questioned in terms of the products or results of the education provided as well as the intentions. Along with this questioning, one can recognize that for some education has been a means of social mobility in the United States with the democratization to a fair extent of the educational capital.

A fifth area in which political structures affect education is the legitimacy and accountability of those who have power to make decisions. Every society needs norms to guide its educational system and provide for continuity as well as change. Persons who work within that system need to be accountable or responsible for the common good. The legislative, executive, and judicial branches of governmental bodies provide some oversight and a means by which to address breaches of responsibility. But some source other than recognized political bodies needs to supply critical evaluation. When it functions best in a democratic society, a free press can provide this need for critical evaluation. In addition, the church can serve as an advocate and evaluator of political policies and activities.

Conclusion

In naming the various educational structures, educators must recognize the interactions that exist among the diverse participants and the unique role that individuals play as they navigate their educational pilgrimage. Because of the need for mere survival that prevails in many communities across the globe, not all persons have the privilege of self-direction. These communities are not limited to developing nations, but include increasing numbers in developed nations such as the United States where persons are identified as members of the "permanent underclass."

Cremin has suggested that the educational effects of these structures, institutions, or agencies can be classified as confirming, complementing, or contradicting one another.[31] In a modern urban pluralistic society the possibility for contradiction and conflict among the various educational structures has increased and at times the greater need is for finding a place for a unity among persons that is not uniformity. Increased diversity for persons in relation to educational options poses the challenge of choice and orchestration of the effects imposed by the various structures considered in this chapter. The search for a workable complementarity that effectively handles the fragmentation, contradictions, and conflicts in modern life and education must be a high priority at the beginning of the third millennium.

In addressing the educational realities of modern life, Cremin referred to a cacophony of teaching—a description of the effects from a variety of educational structures. With such a variety, the ecology of education has been transformed. How then can we teach with such a transformation having occurred in society? Cremin suggests eight insights that serve to dispel traditional educational myths:

1. The longstanding notion that the same teaching always has the same or similar effects on all learners is simply not true.
2. The common notion that teaching is unidirectional from parent to child, from instructor to pupil, from expert to novice is at best simplistic.
3. The social structure of the teaching situation is not in and of itself decisive with respect to the character of what is taught and learned. Some single-parent families may nurture children in ways better than two-parent families.

31. Lawrence A. Cremin, *Public Education* (New York: Basic, 1976), 31; and Lawrence A. Cremin, *Traditions of American Education* (New York: Basic, 1977), 128.

4. The influence of any particular educative structure is rarely direct and unalloyed; it is almost always mediated—that is, reflected, refracted, and interpreted—by other educative structures. The family is probably the most important of these mediating agencies.
5. Neither the processes of teaching and learning in these educative structures nor the character and significance of what is learned are all of a piece. The essence of a good deal of familial education is informal instruction, modeling, explaining, and correcting. The essence of most school education is systematic instruction.
6. Any one of the many institutions that educate can be the decisive influence in the life of an individual, depending upon personality, circumstance, and destiny.
7. Everything that needs to be learned does not necessarily have to be taught or taught in a particular place in a particular time.
8. There is a considerable difference between academic knowledge and everyday knowledge, between the knowledge taught and valued in school and the knowledge needed and valued in everyday life.[32]

Cremin's insights provide a helpful perspective for dealing with educational structures at the end of the twentieth century and for considering the response of Christians.

Having explored the fascinating web of educational structures in this chapter, we must return to questions of educational content with an awareness of how a complex educational context affects decisions with regard to practice. Where we are situated in our teaching ministry and how we work with various institutions that educate will make a difference in our choices of what to teach and how we flesh out our principles. The discussion of educational structures in this chapter pointed up the need to consider the connections across the various institutions that educate in modern society. Chapter 4 will explore educational content in relation to a concern for connection.

32. Lawrence A. Cremin, *Popular Education and Its Discontents* (New York: Harper and Row, 1990), 60–65.

4

Educational Content

Decisions with regard to educational content in Christian education must involve a conscious effort to connect the tasks of the church, namely, proclamation, community, service, advocacy, and worship. Without such a connection, Christians practice a reductionistic, fragmented, and truncated form of education. The challenge in making decisions about content and in effectively communicating that content so that participants holistically embrace it, is to link a focus on content with the complementary foci of persons and context. Such a linking effort is implicit in my definition of education as the process of sharing content with persons in the context of their community and society. The description of a holistic model (chap. 1) and an organizing principle for Christian education (chap. 2), along with the discussion of educational structures (chap. 3), contribute to an understanding of this linkage. An extended discussion of the nature of persons in Christian education is not pursued in this text, but implied throughout the text is sensitivity to the development and needs of persons is required for effective education.[1]

1. For a helpful discussion of the place of persons and our understanding of human development in Christian education see Les Steele, *On the Way: A Practical Theology of Christian Formation* (Grand Rapids: Baker, 1990).

In discussing educational content, educators draw upon their understanding of curricular foundations.[2] From these foundations one can define educational content as that which is shared with participants in teaching. The content, as Lawrence A. Cremin suggests, can include "knowledge, attitudes, values, skills or sensibilities as well as any outcomes of that effort" to share.[3] The content includes not only cognitive material, but also affective and behavioral or lifestyle material. Moreover, content is not just what the teacher intends, but also what the participants actually receive as a result of the teaching, which may be quite different from the teacher's intentions. Cremin suggests this in naming "any outcomes of that effort." It is often the unintended outcomes of teaching that participants or students retain over the years. Educators have sought to recognize this fact by making distinctions between the explicit, hidden, and null curricula, all of which operate in any educational effort. The exploration of the content of each of these three curricula will assist in understanding the choices that are made in teaching. Curriculum can be defined as content made available to students and their actual learning experiences guided by a teacher.[4] This definition suggests that the teacher must assume responsibility for content and experience in the planning, practice, and evaluation of teaching.

In Christian education the teacher must recognize that the ultimate teacher is God and that all of life makes up the curriculum, not just that material identified as appropriate content for consideration. With this recognition comes an awareness of the complexity of teaching and a challenge to faith that affirms God's grace as sufficient to the human needs of both teachers and students alike. As Douglas Wilson observed,

2. For an introduction to curricular foundations, see Robert W. Pazmiño, *Foundational Issues in Christian Education: An Introduction in Evangelical Perspective* (Grand Rapids: Baker, 1988), 205–21.

3. Lawrence A. Cremin named these elements in his definition of education. See *Traditions of American Education* (New York: Basic, 1977), 134.

4. For a more extended discussion of the definition of curriculum see Pazmiño, *Foundational Issues*, 205–7.

"Christian education prepares the way for the grace of God, and it follows up the grace of God. *It does not replace it* [emphasis added]."[5] This recognition also implies an openness to and expectation of the presence and work of the Holy Spirit in the ministry of teaching. While celebrating the mystery of God's work in the teaching of life's content, teachers must exercise care and diligence in areas of the explicit, hidden, and null curricula.

Explicit Curriculum

Elliot Eisner in *The Educational Imagination* makes a helpful distinction between the explicit and the implicit curricula in teaching. The explicit curriculum comprises the stated and planned events that are intended to yield certain educational consequences. It is public and its goals or objectives are commonly understood by those who are participating. The explicit curriculum generally consists of published or printed materials, or descriptions stated in a catalog or syllabus. By contrast, the implicit or hidden curriculum includes the sociological and psychological dimensions of education, which are usually caught rather than intentionally taught. Aspects of the hidden curriculum include the nature of behaviors fostered, compliant or initiative; the type of relationships modeled, competitive or cooperative; and the values emphasized in the community, such as the Christian values of faith, hope, love, truth, peace, joy, and justice. The null curriculum, according to Eisner, is what is not taught. It can be as important as what is taught because it affects the kinds of options one is able to consider, the alternatives that one can examine, and the perspectives from which one can view a situation or a problem. Two major dimensions of the null curriculum are the intellectual processes that are promoted or neglected and the subject areas that are present or absent. The challenge posed with the null curriculum is for teachers to make conscious efforts to structure curriculum so that omissions will be purposeful

5. Douglas Wilson, *Recovering the Lost Tools of Learning: An Approach to Distinctly Christian Education* (Wheaton: Crossway, 1991), 76.

rather than irresponsibly allowed.[6] What then can be proposed in relation to the explicit curriculum or content for Christian education?

The content for Christian education must focus upon the five tasks of the church (using the model in chap. 3) and enable students to see and embrace the vital unity that exists across these tasks. Seeing and embracing this unity explicitly is crucial in a time when life itself and the Christian life are often perceived and experienced as fragmented. This fragmentation is a characteristic of modern urbanized life at the dawn of the twenty-first century and calls for a creative response on the part of the Christian church.

In relationship to the model of the five tasks of proclamation, community, service, advocacy, and worship, one can connect the tasks in ten ways (see fig. 4):

1. Community and proclamation
2. Community and worship
3. Community and service
4. Worship and proclamation
5. Worship and service
6. Service and proclamation
7. Service and advocacy
8. Advocacy and worship
9. Advocacy and community
10. Advocacy and proclamation

These ten linkages stress the need for teachers to foster a vital connection for Christians through the explicit curriculum or

6. Elliot W. Eisner, *The Educational Imagination: On the Design and Evaluation of School Programs,* 2d ed. (New York: Macmillan, 1985), 87–107. Beyond Ronald T. Habermas's discussion of the null curriculum in "Even What You Don't Say Counts," *Christian Education Journal* 5 (Autumn 1984): 24–27, he has suggested two additional ways of analyzing the null curriculum. It is possible to conceive of the explicit-null curriculum as the intentional omissions and the implicit-null curriculum as the unintentional omissions. An example of the former in a local church might be the absence of discussions of such controversial subjects as evolution. An example of the latter might be the absence of advocacy ministries for such persons as AIDS victims. Both types of omissions have powerful effects on a curriculum and the options provided for participants.

Figure 4
Connections between the Five Tasks

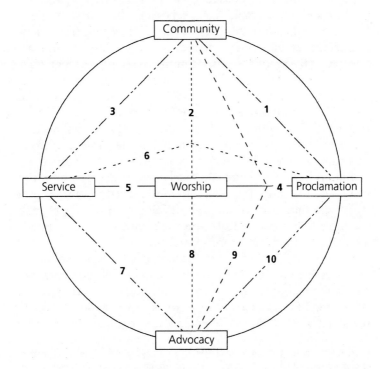

content of Christian education. Such an analysis is intended not to lead to a rigid or highly structured design for teaching and learning, but to encourage the careful and sensitive weaving together of the gospel demands within the life of the Christian community. These links also provide a means by which to assess the educational diet of any particular community and to discern particulars of the explicit, implicit, and null curricula that need attention. Where gaps exist, Christian educators can plan for specific curricular emphases and themes that complement the existing efforts. For example, a local church may be effectively teaching biblical content (proclamation) to all ages in the Sunday school program (community) and thus effectively linking community and proclamation.[7] But this same community may not be adequately encouraging persons to actively engage in service within and outside the local church. This situation suggests the need for a renewed emphasis on service in the Christian life by explicit teaching or training about various opportunities to serve (connecting service and proclamation), by commissioning and celebrating the service of persons in the congregation (connecting service and worship), and by advocating the active service and mission in the faithful response of God's people to the gospel of Jesus Christ (connecting advocacy and service).

For each link educators can identify an educational need:

Community and proclamation. All participants in a Christian education program need to know the common story of the Christian faith, to commit themselves to participation in that story, and to draw a sense of corporate identity from the faith story being proclaimed through developmentally appropriate teaching. Many evangelical churches have effectively trained a biblically literate faith community.

Community and worship. Persons need to understand the meaning of Christian worship and the nature of their corporate and individual participation in celebrating their faith through the liturgy. Liturgy refers to the work of the people in public worship.[8] The whole people of God need to be active in corpo-

7. A legitimate question to raise is whether all ages need all the combinations or connections equally or whether certain combinations are more critical per age development and needs—that is, the question of learning readiness and development. A response to such an inquiry must consider the educational diet and contextual factors that relate to a particular group of learners. Discernment is related to the educational trinity proposed in this work. First, one must be sensitive to the developmental needs of persons so that the teaching is psychologically appropriate. Second, one must be sensitive to the nature of the content so that the teaching is logically appropriate. Third, one must sensitive to the nature of the context, the community, and the society in which one is teaching, so that the teaching is historically, culturally, and sociologically appropriate. All such considerations are subject to biblical, theological, and philosophical commitments and scrutiny.

8. Horace Allen, "Liturgy as Hermeneutic: Scripture and Sacrament" (lecture at Andover Newton Theological School, Newton Centre, Mass., 17 March 1992), defines liturgy as a playful participation in the Bible's world of sign and story. Thus the work of liturgy includes play, which children can best exemplify for adults.

rate worship, which is one expression of their loving response to God and their reasonable service. This understanding is not limited to cognitive and abstract concepts, but includes the intuitive, experiential, and emotional participation of children, youth, and adults who gather to honor and revere the presence of God in their lives. The educational need is to foster a greater appreciation and depth of meaning and feeling that persons can gain through worship as a community. One particular challenge for many congregations is the extent to which children and youth are welcome in corporate worship and encouraged to actively participate.[9]

Community and service. Persons need to name their gifts, talents, and responsibilities and to understand how these gifts can best be used within the church. People need opportunities for the training, support, and expression of their gifts. This may require careful coordination and creating a network of persons who can serve as mentors to others in various ministries. The goal is to develop a symphony of service for the common good of humanity and all of creation and to foster the recognition of vital ministries in the life of the faith community.

Worship and proclamation. The need is to associate the reenactment of the Christian story in symbols and cymbals to the good news of God's past, present, and future activities on behalf of humankind. Public worship reenacts the great accounts of the Christian story in contemporary life. The challenge is for people to discern the intent of God's promises and demands in fresh images and then to respond through corporate and individual worship. This response calls us to love God with all of our heart, soul, mind, and strength, and to love our neighbor. For such a response to occur, persons need to perceive the Christian story as a way of making sense of life today. They need to know the Christian story in all of its breadth and depth, and this calls for a lifelong commitment to study and wrestle with the meaning of the gospel. It also calls for the response of joyful hearts and lives to the manifold grace of God in Jesus Christ made possible by the work of the Holy Spirit. By linking worship and proclamation, individuals are better able to meaning-

9. For an exploration of this issue see David Ng and Virginia Thomas, *Children in the Worshiping Community* (Atlanta: John Knox, 1981).

fully participate in corporate gatherings, having gained some biblical and theological literacy.

Worship and service. Worship can prepare people for service. God empowers and enables individuals to serve and calls them to specific areas of service within the larger claims of Christian vocation. In worship God refreshes and renews persons so they can sustain their activity in the world and launch new ventures in faith. In worship Christians can relate their activities to God's eternal creative and redemptive activities because it is God's mission in which they are called to participate. It is through worship that persons are empowered to better serve and fulfill their unique calling. The educational need implied in this connection is the transformation of perspective that enables persons to interpret their activities in relation to the call of God. One's work in the world can thus be seen as a ministry with God to serve God, others, and the creation. That service may take place in the home, in the community, in the workplace, or in the church as it gathers.

Service and proclamation. Christians are called to proclaim the Christian story through their deeds, through the witness of actions, which can speak louder than words. The educational need in this connection is to pose the question asked in the Book of James, which stresses the connection between faith and works. This emphasis is also present throughout the Pauline epistles: If the gospel indicates a truth to be affirmed, a command follows that provides guidelines for faithful response. This educational connection does not imply a stance of either conditioning or indoctrination understood in a pejorative sense. Thoughts and behaviors are not imposed and so narrowly described as to eliminate careful thought and decision by participants. But the act of knowing in a biblical sense implies a predisposition to act in ways consistent with that knowledge.

Service and advocacy. Christian educators are called to be advocates of the need for Christians to serve and to incarnate God's creative and redemptive mission of reconciliation, peace, justice, and joy in the world. The advocacy of needs in the larger society provides occasions for Christians to explore areas for service that were not apparent in earlier times. One example of such a need is the rise in the numbers of "latchkey children."

In response, a number of churches have initiated after-school care for these children. Other churches supply preschool nursery and day-care services for children whose working parents or extended family cannot do so.

Advocacy and worship. This connection suggests the need to celebrate renewed symbols in liturgy that raise questions about our faithfulness to the gospel. The worship experience can pose problems we have forgotten and suggest resources in God and in our faith to respond faithfully. A footwashing ceremony in some churches could symbolize a move to renewal in addressing larger social issues and to advocate for the needs of persons who have been forgotten. On a more practical level, the need is to raise the consciousness of worshipers regarding situations in the community, the wider society, and across the globe that call for a Christian response of social action and/or witness.

Advocacy and community. The connection between advocacy and community embodies the tension between what we are called to be as the people of God and what we have become. The educational need is to suggest alternatives to the community and to care enough to confront the community, to speak the truth in love when and where it is necessary. This confrontation must be constructive, to allow for the reconciliation if at all possible. Where reconciliation is not possible, Christians may need to explore the option of agreeing to disagree. The challenge is to speak the truth in love and not to refrain from naming God's judgment upon the community's disparities and sins. Advocacy in relation to the community raises the possibility of conflict not only within the faith community, but also between the local church and the wider community or society. By not accommodating the Christian faith to the dominant culture, Christians are subject to the rejection and persecution that Jesus himself encountered in his earthly ministry. The community must be prepared for the costs involved in advocacy. I witnessed the costs that a local church experienced because of their advocacy of a sanctuary for Central American refugees in Tucson, Arizona.

Advocacy and proclamation. As Christians we are called to be advocates of the vision embodied in the Christian story of

99

God's reign. The vitality of the Christian proclamation is dependent upon its incarnation in the lives of Christians who are called to be advocates for Christ and the gospel's values in society. Susanne Johnson suggests that Christian education links three stories: life story, cultural story, and Christian story.[10] Faithful linking between Christian story (proclamation) and cultural and life stories is possible only as Christians willingly advocate the outworking of Christian values in public life. In the United States, Christians may be tempted to privatize and ghettoize their faith. The educational need in this connection is to develop a public theology that brings the Christian faith to bear upon wider social, political, and economic issues. Not to engage such a challenge results in sectarianism and reductionism of the whole gospel for the whole world. It refrains in practice from affirming the truth that Jesus Christ is Lord.

Explicit curriculum can promote all of the ten connections, but the practical question that remains for a teacher is how to plan for a lesson.

Lesson Planning

Various structures have been proposed to guide teachers in planning lessons. But teachers first need to clarify goals or objectives they hope to accomplish through the teaching itself. The work of Eisner again is helpful in making distinctions that influence teaching and the approach one will take in fostering learning.

Eisner distinguishes three categories of curricular or content objectives: behavioral, problem-solving, and expressive objectives. Behavioral objectives name very specific behaviors that students will be expected to demonstrate at the conclusion of a teaching unit. One example from a Sunday school curriculum might be for junior-age students (grades 5 and 6) to name all the books of the New Testament in order. Problem-solving objectives pose a problem or raise a question for which a number of possible solutions or answers exist. With problem-solving objectives the emphasis is upon exploration and flexibility rather than upon precision. One example of such an objective for juniors would be to plan for a class visit to the home of a bed-ridden child of their age. Expressive

10. Susanne Johnson, *Christian Spiritual Formation in the Church and Classroom* (Nashville: Abingdon, 1989), 90.

100

objectives do not specify explicit or precise goals, but foster the imagination and vision of students by providing the space and time for creative expression.[11] One example of such an activity would be to provide craft materials and art media that allow the junior children to create some expression of their thoughts and feelings about the theme of thanksgiving to God. One can imagine the responses that such an activity might elicit. (Knowing juniors, one must also set some reasonable limits for how expressive activities cannot abuse the materials or others and their work.) Setting the stage for engagement in expressive activities is important in directing student efforts.

In moving from behavioral to problem-solving to expressive objectives, the amount of precision and specificity in teaching outcomes is reduced, but the opportunity for creativity and discovery is increased. In such a progression one is conscious of how teaching can combine insights from the science of education with its precision with insights from the art or craft of education with its creativity. Too many published curricula have relied exclusively upon behavioral objectives, assuming that they alone encompass the content of teaching. To promote a holistic approach, teachers need to adapt the published curricula and plan problem-solving and expressive activities for students.

Beyond the question of goals and objectives teachers have often sought a structure or framework in which to plan their lessons. The work of Lawrence O. Richards and Donald L. Griggs in lesson planning has provided such structure. Richards has suggested an easily remembered framework that includes the four elements of hook, book, look, and took. The hook is an approach to the lesson that draws in and interests the participants. The book is the presentation of a biblical story, theme, or concept. The look is the exploration of the implications and applications of the material for the life of the participants. The took is the suggestion of and commitment to actual responses on the part of participants in the light of what has been learned or discovered.[12] The strength of Richards's structure is its simplicity and its attention to the implications and applications of

11. Eisner, *The Educational Imagination*, 109–25.

12. Lawrence O. Richards, *Creative Bible Teaching* (Chicago: Moody, 1970), 108–13.

content along with participant response. These elements are too readily ignored in the press to share the content, the book, in evangelical educational practice.

Griggs provides a similar structure in naming five elements for lesson planning: opening, presentation, explore subject, creative response, and conclude. The opening parallels Richards's hook and introduces the lesson to the students. The presentation parallels Richards's book, and it can include a film, student input, a story, a puppet play, or an exercise in value clarification. Unlike Richards's structure, which represents a more conservative theological approach, the presentation does not focus exclusively on biblical information. The explore subject element is similar to Richards's look and the creative response parallels Richards's took. Griggs adds the element of conclude, which emphasizes the closure.[13]

The strengths of Griggs's structure are similar to those of Richards's framework and point up some persistent concerns in the organization of a lesson. These concerns include the need to engage and motivate students; to share with them some essential content or enable them to discover content on their own; and students' need to transfer new insights or perspectives to their wider contexts by grappling with implications of, applications of, and responses to the content. Both structures give teachers the means to share content in a way that intersects or connects with the experience of students. But the central focus is upon sharing content while involving the students.

Alternative structures for lesson planning emphasize the other two foci, persons and context, in the educational trinity (chaps. 1 and 2). Thomas H. Groome has proposed an alternative structure, "shared praxis," which includes five movements:

1. Looking at life—participants share their experience on a particular theme by naming their present action.
2. Sharing life—participants share stories and visions and reflect on the experiences shared for connections.
3. Knowing the faith—the teacher shares the Christian community's story and vision on a particular theme.

13. Donald L. Griggs, *Teaching Teachers to Teach: A Basic Manual for Church Teachers* (Nashville: Abingdon, 1974), 17–22.

4. Owning the faith—participants connect the Christian story with their own situations and stories.
5. Living the faith—participants are invited to make decisions and responses that connect the Christian vision with their visions.[14]

Groome's first two movements can be equated with Richards's hook, movement 3 with book, movement 4 with look, and movement 5 with took. But shared praxis generally focuses upon the participants and their context as they engage the lesson's theme. In addition, they are asked to make connections to the content of the Christian faith, the story, and vision. Some variation can be noted in Groome's structure, but it shows a remarkable similarity to the structures of both Richards and Griggs. The underlying, organizing principle that can be discerned in these curricular structures is that of making connections between the content, the persons, and their context. Any holistic approach that seriously engages the educational trinity of content, persons, and context encourages students to make connections.

A second alternative can be explored in the work of Paulo Freire, a Brazilian educator, whose approach to lesson structure centers upon the context of participants and, in particular, their society and its structures of meaning.[15] The focus upon the context follows from Freire's reconstructionist philosophy and his commitment to contextual theology. Freire's innovative methods in his literacy work suggest the following: a thorough search into the situation of the students; the choice of themes for discussion from the situation of the people; a graphic representation of these themes; open discussion on these themes; and a commitment to action on the part of both students and teacher as a result of discussion.[16] One notes in Freire's methodology

14. Thomas H. Groome, *Christian Religious Education: Sharing Our Story and Vision* (San Francisco: Harper and Row, 1980), 207–23.

15. For a brief discussion of Freire's insights for Christian education, see Pazmiño, *Foundational Issues*, 68–72. For more extensive analysis, see Daniel S. Schipani, *Conscientization and Creativity, Paulo Freire and Christian Education* (Lanham, Md.: University Press of America, 1984); and Daniel S. Schipani, *Religious Education Encounters Liberation Theology* (Birmingham, Ala.: Religious Education Press, 1988).

16. John L. Elias, "Paulo Freire: Religious Educator," *Religious Education* 71 (January–February 1976): 55–56.

a remarkable similarity to what Groome later proposed in shared praxis, but with the important difference of Groome's conscious effort to share the Christian story and vision and to be in dialogue with the tradition.

Thus in lesson planning teachers can appropriate diverse structures and entry points and yet recognize the underlying need to share content with persons in the context of their community and society and in so doing to make connections. The different structures place initial emphasis on one of the three elements: content, persons, or context. But each seeks to incorporate the connections required for effective Christian education by linking with the other elements. The predisposition of evangelical educators has been to give priority to content, but much can be learned from approaches that opt for other points of entry. The wisdom shared by Lois E. LeBar in relation to curriculum, though not original to her, applies to this discussion. She noted that in teaching, content without experience is empty and experience without content is blind.[17] Experience can be seen in relation not only to persons, but also to communities and societies. Thus, the key to effective lesson planning is to wed or connect content with the experience of both persons and the wider community and society. In making connections, teachers must recognize the dynamics of the hidden or implicit curriculum and consider aspects of classroom management, teaching style, and creativity.

Hidden Curriculum

The hidden curriculum represents as much a responsibility of the Christian teacher as that of the explicit curriculum. The ten possible connections in relation to the explicit curriculum may take on the character of being implicit or hidden when the personal relationships and social structures themselves foster the necessary linking of tasks. One must also recognize the unique work of the Holy Spirit in enabling persons to perceive the interconnections of faith and life that characterize teaching in a faith community. What this implies for the Christian

17. Lois E. LeBar, "Curriculum," in *An Introduction to Evangelical Christian Education,* ed. J. Edward Hakes (Chicago: Moody, 1964), 89.

teacher is openness to the moving and work of the Holy Spirit through the hidden curriculum and the creation of space for expressive activities as a too often neglected goal of the explicit curriculum. Whereas consideration of the explicit curriculum tends to be preoccupied with content, consideration of the implicit or hidden curriculum tends to be preoccupied with persons and context.

Classroom Management

A matter of constant concern and attention in a number of Christian education programs is that of discipline. In an undisciplined age questioning authority, even legitimate authority, is the norm. Questioning authority may often be legitimate, given the common experience of abuse, oppression, and injustice at the hands of those with authority in society. But the general climate of distrust and autonomy in relation to authority is not consistent with a Christian world view. The Christian life involves discipline and a clear call to discipleship before God and others as an outworking of that discipline. Discipleship in the Christian life, according to the work of Marianne Sawicki, entails four elements: a personal encounter with Jesus, a clear call to which one responds, a mission to testify to others about Jesus, and following Jesus to death.[18] These four elements need to be expanded upon in relation to the discipline of the Christian community itself, which serves to elaborate upon the nature of the call, mission, and following that Sawicki names. This corporate or communal discipline can be understood in relation to the five tasks of the church, proclamation, community, service, advocacy, and worship.

The overarching principle in classroom management is to balance a concern for discipline with a concern for creativity, to balance form and freedom. Some settings can so stress discipline and structure that creative expression is squelched. The corresponding danger is to so stress freedom and expression that no limits or structures are provided. The general educational wisdom is to begin any class with the clear articulation of guidelines, of a structure in which students can sense security and

18. Marianne Sawicki, *The Gospel in History: Portrait of a Teaching Church, The Origins of Christian Education* (New York: Paulist, 1988), 60, 62, 90.

learn. Once such structure is initially established and often tested, then the opportunity for expression and appropriate freedom can be explored. But in Christian life the question must be posed: Freedom for what? The answer of the gospel is freedom to serve, freedom to be and become a faithful disciple of Jesus Christ in the church and in the world. The implied question, of course, is: Freedom from what? The response of the gospel has been freedom from sin, both corporate and personal. Classroom management must be seen as a necessary restraint upon the human disposition to sin, along with the corresponding encouragement of the appropriate exercise of the human freedom to serve God and others.

One key to addressing discipline problems is an initial clear statement of guidelines for behavior and of consequences that follow from any breach of the guidelines. Clarity about and the opportunity to discuss guidelines foster their ownership on the part of participants. This assumes that responsible teachers are willing to model appropriate behavior themselves and care enough to confront problems when they emerge. This key is popularly identified as starting out tough and then loosening up as time passes and guidelines are adopted by the group.

A second key to effective discipline is planning developmentally appropriate learning activities for students that make use of both the teacher's and students' creativity. Active and challenging participation deters discipline problems.

A third key is the difficult challenge of correcting behavior without rejecting the person manifesting the inappropriate behavior. This is captured in the popular expression "loving the sinner, but hating the sin." For this to be effective, teachers need to sense that they are in fact being supported by those who administer any program and that they have recourse if a difficult confrontation should arise. Avoiding repeated discipline problems requires a sensitive discernment of what is at stake and a commitment to be in responsible relationship with others. Part of that discernment in recent years has involved the consideration of teaching and learning styles.

106

Teaching and Learning Styles

Teaching is a matter of style. Learning is a matter of style. Style is what one is, and in the Christian faith, what one is in Christ. Style is the image of one's character, which for the Christian is to reflect the character of Christ. Thus the development of the art of teaching must be seen in relation to personality and character as well as to the explicit content of teaching, teaching techniques, and teaching skills. Teachers must grapple with who they are and whose they are in the acts of teaching. "Who they are" refers to unique personal characteristics, gifts, and sensitivities. "Whose they are" refers to the quality of their relationship to God. Developing an effective teaching style and supporting the learning styles represented in any group of learners are achieved by loving and artful attention to particulars of what one is and does, both as a person and as a teacher. This loving and artful attention must also include the nature of one's relationship with God, with the assumption that God is the ultimate teacher in Christian teaching.

Most descriptions of learning and teaching styles have identified four distinctive styles:

1. Innovative learners/teachers, sensing-feelers, divergers—These persons learn by listening and sharing ideas. They are divergent in their interests and thoughts, connecting with a wide variety of persons and things. They stress what they perceive or see and then generalize. They tend to be warm and interpersonal in their relationships. As teachers, these persons are nurturers, supporters, and empathizers.
2. Common-sense learners/teachers, sensing-thinkers, convergers—These people enjoy taking what they have learned and trying to build something experimental. As learners they do not value the teacher's input; they are trying things out and experimenting with their own perceptions and thoughts. They are realistic, practical, and pragmatic. They are convergent in their thoughts, relating ideas to reality and actual practice. As teachers, these persons are trainers, information givers, and instructional managers.

107

3. Analytic learners/teachers, intuitive-thinkers, assimilators—These people enjoy learning by listening to a teacher lecture. They are the thinkers and watchers in classes, and their thinking patterns are rational and sequential. They can assimilate a wide variety of insights into comprehensive and holistic concepts or images. As teachers these persons are intellectual challengers, theoreticians, and inquirers who honor the place of intuition and integration.

4. Dynamic learners/teachers, intuitive-feelers, accommodators—These people enjoy taking what they have learned and using their imagination and curiosity to build something experimental and new from it. They start with what they can see, hear, touch, and feel, but then create new combinations and possibilities to accommodate a wide variety of insights and persons in their efforts. Dynamic learners need to be given adequate space and flexibility and may express distinctive attitudes and behavior. As teachers these persons are facilitators, stimulators, and creators who encourage others to be active and to explore making use of their creativity.[19]

Any individual may incorporate a variety of these styles, but many have a dominant or a preferred style from which they learn and teach. Insights from a style inventory or description can help in the effort to individualize learning, but the greater challenge is to incorporate a variety of styles or to teach from one's dominant style, while allowing for a degree of flexibility to accommodate the learning styles that are generally represented in any given group of learners. But the stress upon variety, which is my predisposition, may deprive learners of essential learning in depth within any one style. Maria Harris argues for the understanding of teaching in relation to a learning circle

19. For some basic descriptions of these categories, see Marlene D. LeFever, "Learning Styles: Not All Kids Learn in the Same Way," *Foundations* (Spring/Summer 1986); Bernice McCarthy, *The 4Mat System* (Barrington, Ill.: Excel, n.d.); and Harvey F. Silver and Robert J. Hanson, *Teaching Styles and Strategies* (Moorestown, N.J.: Hanson Silver & Associates, 1982).

that intentionally incorporates dimensions of learning across the four general categories of style. She names the inclusion of concrete experience (preferred by dynamic and innovative learners), reflective observation (preferred by innovative and analytic learners), abstract conceptualization (preferred by analytic and common-sense learners), and active experimentation (preferred by common-sense and dynamic learners).[20] But teachers with highly developed styles may concentrate on limited segments of Harris's learning circle. Harris thus encourages breadth in teaching rather than depth exploration of any one style. The discipline or subject in which one is teaching along with the age level of students may affect the choice of breadth over depth in relation to learning styles.

Historically, it is important to note that a discussion of style is not just a modern interest. Augustine identified three styles of communication. The first, a subdued style, serves for instruction when the intent is to teach intellectual material. The second, an elegant style, serves for praise when the intent is to delight persons and God. The third, a majestic style, serves for exhortation when the intent is to move persons to commitment and action. According to Augustine's thought, it is possible to combine all three styles with the same end in view. That end is to bring home the truth to the hearers, so that they may understand it, hear it with gladness, and practice it in their lives.[21] Augustine's insights are a corrective to the modern preoccupation with the personal assessment of style to the exclusion of the greater end of teaching. That greater end is to glorify and enjoy God forever. Glorifying and enjoying God include the opportunity to express one's creativity as a teacher and as a student, which is the next area of the hidden curriculum to consider.

Creativity

> To do all the things we have forgotten . . . to walk on
> water . . . to speak to the angels who call us . . . to

20. Maria Harris, *Teaching and Religious Imagination: An Essay in the Theology of Teaching* (San Francisco: Harper and Row, 1987), 43–46.
21. Augustine "On Christian Doctrine" 4.1–30, in *A Select Library of the Nicene and Post-Nicene Fathers of the Christian Church,* ed. Philip Schaff (Grand Rapids: Eerdmans, 1979), 574–97.

> move unfettered, among the stars . . . listening for
> meaning, feeling for healing . . . glimpses of the world
> of the other of space and time . . . glimpses of glory . . .
> creativity opens us to revelation.[22]

So Madeline L'Engle defines creativity, and her associations suggest that our creativity reflects God's creativity and our creation in God's image. Creativity opens us to revelation, God's revelation, as we acknowledge the place of mystery, wonder, joy, and awe in our lives as teachers and students in the process of teaching. Every person has creative abilities that can find expression through teaching. Ethné Gray, an artist who teaches, has observed that the truth is not so much that every artist is a special kind of person, but that every person is a special kind of artist. The challenge posed in the hidden curriculum is to not squelch the creativity of teachers or students and to nurture the artistry in every person.

Marlene LeFever, who has explored creativity in relation to teaching, sees creativity as including the ability to invent or innovate, the ability to evaluate critically, and esthetic sensitivity and flexibility.[23] This descriptive definition suggests that every teacher has some creative ability that can be exercised and that every teacher can encourage the creative expression of students through the choice of appropriate methods and the cultivation of students' abilities. Creativity takes a variety of forms and everyone has some imaginative capacity that can be used to the glory of God and for the enjoyment of others through teaching and learning. LeFever explores creative teaching methods that all teachers can practice and demonstrates this possibility in *Creative Teaching Methods*.

Donald L. Griggs provides a third definition of creativity: "Any thinking or planning process which solves a problem in an original and useful way."[24] This definition suggests that teach-

22. Madeleine L'Engle uses these phrases throughout *Walking on Water: Reflections on Faith and Art* (Wheaton: Harold Shaw, 1980).

23. Marlene D. LeFever, *Growing Creative Children* (Wheaton: Tyndale House, 1981), 11. Also see her *Creative Teaching Methods* (Elgin, Ill.: David C. Cook, 1985).

24. Donald L. Griggs, *Basic Teacher Skills for Church Teachers* (Nashville: Abingdon, 1985), 66.

ers can actually foster a process that encourages creativity, and Griggs lists the factors that encourage creativity:

1. An open, inviting environment
2. A focus on problem solving rather than on answer giving
3. Opportunities to make choices
4. Time to experiment or warm up
5. Need for acceptance and respect[25]

These factors are aspects of the hidden curriculum that require the careful attention of teachers who seek not only to be creative themselves, but also to foster the creativity of their students. Plato observed that what is honored in a country is cultivated there. Honoring creativity will result in cultivating it through the implicit curriculum. To cultivate creativity entails reserving time and space in the explicit curriculum for creative exploration and expression. The most common experience in teaching is that so much content is shared at the metaphoric table that students have little or no time to chew and digest the food—that is, to discuss and connect the content. Participants need time and space to playfully explore new ways in which to appropriate the content into their lives and to transfer the insights shared to other areas, making possible meaningful integration.

"The simplest definition of art is the activity by which people realize the place of ideals in their lives."[26] Christians need to nurture the art of teaching through honoring creativity. Christians need to relish the ideals of the Christian faith in passing it on to current and future generations. Christians need to delight in the Lord Jesus Christ and to teach in ways that communicate that joy through a vast variety of creative approaches and methods. The nurturing of creativity also helps avoid the discipline problems mentioned earlier.

25. Ibid., 69.
26. This quote from Howard Thurman is noted by Ronald Gariboldi and Daniel Novotny, *The Art of Theological Reflection: An Ecumenical Study* (Lanham, Md.: University Press of America, 1987), 100.

Null Curriculum

The null curriculum is one that is not often considered in the discussion of educational content, with some notable exceptions.[27] But it must be considered, as Harris notes:

> The null curriculum is a paradox. This is the curriculum that exists because it does not exist; it is what is left out. But the point of including it is that ignorance or the absence of something is not neutral. It skews the balance of options we might consider, alternatives from which we might choose, or perspectives that help us see. The null curriculum includes areas left out (content, themes, points of view) and procedures left unused (the arts, play, critical analysis). The implicit curriculum, in contrast, does not leave out areas and procedures. It simply does not call them to attention. They are there, operative in the situation but left unnoticed.[28]

With its paradoxical nature, the null curriculum may be difficult to discern, except when a conscious effort is made to consider what has been forgotten. Discernment of what is left out occurs by developing a comprehensive vision of Christian education and of the ideals that Howard Thurman named. This vision and corresponding ideals do not lead to impractical speculation, but to careful assessment of the experience of education itself in the light of the ends of which Augustine reminds us. In other words, the most practical of all things in discerning the nature and character of the explicit, implicit, and null curricula for teaching is a good theory. A good theory helps name all the elements and to see the necessary connections in the effort to be faithful in the ministries of Christian education and in all other ministries.

The educational trinity and the five-task model of Christian education are components of an educational theory that help discern what the null curriculum is in any educational setting. For example, an educational program may so stress content con-

27. See the works of Ronald T. Habermas, "Even What You Don't Say Counts," *Christian Education Journal* 5 (Autumn 1984): 24–27; and Maria Harris, *Fashion Me a People: Curriculum in the Church* (Louisville: Westminster/John Knox, 1989), 69, 122, 174.
28. Harris, *Fashion Me a People*, 69.

siderations as to exclude adequate consideration of the unique character of the persons participating and their developmental needs and interests. The place of persons and individualizing their learning to enable personal appropriation would then be the null curriculum (along with adequate consideration of the context). An illustration of this in Christian education curriculum is the general practice of translating materials written in English for suburban English-speaking middle-class churches directly into Spanish for use in urban working-class Hispanic churches without modifying the cultural context.

As a second example, another educational program may focus so exclusively upon the individual needs of participants and fostering their growth that no consideration is given to sharing adequate content in a direct and transformative way and no consideration is given to issues in the wider community and society beyond personal and introspective needs. In this case the null curriculum would be elements of content and the connection with the context. An illustration of this in Christian-education curriculum is the use of experience-based introspective material that has participants share their personal feelings and thoughts to the exclusion of any biblical or theological content. Participants often call this experience pooled ignorance, which fails to explore one's relationships to others and the wider community and society.

A third educational program could so focus on the place of the community/society (either to prepare persons to conform to or to transform the particular community/society) that it ignores content or the unique character of the participants and the ways in which they can conform to and/or transform their context. An illustration of this in Christian education curriculum is material that exclusively addresses a current burning issue in the community or society without exploring how students view or even own the issue. This material also does not gain the perspective provided by the Christian tradition for understanding the issue in light of historical examples, but rather has participants conform to the current proposed perception and agenda. In the effort to follow a trend and to be contemporary in either accommodating to or rejecting the status quo, participants gain little perspective from their faith or personal appropriation of it.

The ten possible connections in relation to the explicit curriculum serve as means by which to discern what has been forgotten and therefore, needs nurture in order for teachers to be faithful in the work of Christian education. By noting the null curriculum, teachers can plan alternatives and implement processes that address the gaps. For example, a gap that has become increasingly apparent in some evangelical churches involves few connections being made with the tasks of service and advocacy. To address this, Christian educators should attempt to plan specific events that expose and train persons for service and that address advocacy issues in relating the Christian faith to the wider society. Advocacy issues might be explored in relation to the formation of a public theology. Max L. Stackhouse in *Public Theology and Political Economy* suggests ten concepts essential for developing public theology: Creation, liberation, vocation, covenant, moral law, sin, freedom, ecclesiology, the Trinity, and Christology.[29] These concepts and others could become the agenda for adult study in relation to public issues and Christian response. The stress upon a public theology can confront the potential weaknesses in evangelicalism of individualism, ghettoism, sectarianism, and privatism, which Donald G. Bloesch named.[30] These weaknesses can coalesce in evangelical churches and result in a hidden or even explicit curriculum that stresses isolation and separation from the public realm. The resulting null curriculum is the absence of discussion of crucial public issues in the curriculum and no development of critical Christian social analysis. Bible passages that address the public sphere, such as Deuteronomy 15:7–11, Psalm 72:1–4, 12–14, or Isaiah 58, are not studied or related to Christians' public responsibilities. Other possibilities could be imagined if the null curriculum is addressed, and we are willing to respond creatively to new challenges.

29. Max L. Stackhouse, *Public Theology and Political Economy* (Grand Rapids: Eerdmans, 1987), 94.
30. See chap. 1, n. 1.

Conclusion

This chapter has sought to explore educational content and to provide some useful categories to guide Christian educators in their ministries. The areas of the explicit, hidden, and null curricula were discussed in order to provide teachers with specific insights on how the use of the educational trinity and five-task model in planning and implementing a comprehensive curriculum. The organizing principle stressed is making connections that incorporate the content and experience of persons and communities who seek to be faithful to the gospel of Jesus Christ. The discussion of educational content must be related to questions of educational methods, which were mentioned in passing but are the focus of chapter 5.

5

Educational Methods

The choice of educational methods requires a clear understanding of teaching and learning. However, both are defined differently from a wide variety of perspectives. The problem is further complicated by current research that identifies a variety of teaching styles and learning styles at work in any educational setting, and these combine in infinite complexity. No wonder many educators feel overwhelmed as they search for principles to guide them in the choice of methods. In an attempt to establish some order, I offer the following definitions and principles.

A View of Teaching

In recent discussions of education, the emphasis has been upon learning. It is, however, my contention that teaching is at the heart of education.[1] Lucien E. Coleman defines teaching as "a process in which a person engages in actions intended to help another person learn."[2] In this definition "process" denotes a

1. Mary C. Boys elaborates upon the theme "Teaching: The Heart of Religious Education," *Religious Education* 79 (Spring 1984): 252–72.
2. Lucien E. Coleman, Jr., "The Meaning of Teaching," in *The Ministry of Religious Education*, comp. John T. Sisemore (Nashville: Broadman, 1978), 52.

dynamic interaction and an ongoing relationship between persons over time. It also implies that the process is systematic or sustained over time. A "person" assumes a human agent or agents who are involved in planning, implementing, or evaluating the process. "Engages in actions" suggests that the teacher is active and exercising initiative. "Intended" denotes that teaching is purposeful and deliberate. It also suggests that the teacher is able to identify intentions either explicitly or implicitly when questioned. "To help another person learn" suggests that learning is the intended result of teaching and that the final responsibility and work in learning belongs to the student.[3] No teacher can guarantee learning, but effective teaching may encourage cooperation from the student that results in learning.

Coleman's activist understanding of teaching is balanced by Parker J. Palmer, in *To Know as We Are Known*. He defines teaching as "creating a space in which obedience to truth is practiced."[4] Whereas activity is involved in creating a space, receptivity is also required in order to maintain a space that is not inappropriately filled with content. Such receptivity implies opportunities or space for teachers to listen and for students to discuss content. This space, from a Christian perspective, allows participants to respond in obedience to God's truth, discerned through the living, written, and created Word of God. This further elaboration of Palmer's definition raises a key question: What are the distinctive characteristics of teaching in a Christian sense?

Brian Hill, an Australian educator, suggests that Christian teaching can in some measure be distinguished from general teaching in terms of its content, manner, and context. The content of Christian teaching is the moral and spiritual revelation of God. Its manner is both instruction and admonition: instruction in the sense of informing students of God's truth, and admonition in the sense of challenging the students' way of life. The context of Christian teaching is nurture within the community of faith or direct outreach beyond it.[5] In other words,

3. Ibid., 52–53.
4. Parker J. Palmer, *To Know as We Are Known: A Spirituality of Education* (San Francisco: Harper and Row, 1983), 69.
5. Brian Hill, *Faith at the Blackboard: Issues Facing the Christian Teacher* (Grand Rapids: Eerdmans, 1982), 74–76.

teaching in the Christian sense is proclaiming God's requirements of persons, handing down the content of the Christian
faith, drawing out implications for the personal and corporate
lives of students and teachers, and calling for decision and
response.

Coleman, Palmer, and Hill provide insights for understanding
Christian teaching. The Christian teacher participates in actions
intended to help students learn about God's revelation and
requirements. This is the handing down or transmission of the
content of the Christian faith and the reappropriation of that
content in the light of contemporary challenges. Likewise, the
Christian teacher creates a space in which obedience to God's
truth is practiced. It is not sufficient to pass down and reinter-
pret the content without struggling with its implications for
the lives of students and without calling for decision and
response on the part of all participants. For this to occur in
teaching, more than proclamation or transmission is implied.
Dialogue and interaction are necessary if students are to appropriate and apply truth. All too frequently Christian churches
have chosen one or the other of these emphases in teaching.
This imbalance has led to exclusive emphases on either orthodoxy, right content, or orthopraxis, right practice or living.
Christian teaching assumes an adequate grappling with both
dimensions of Christian faith, orthodoxy and orthopraxis. An
exclusive emphasis on orthodoxy often results in disregard for
the implications of God's truth for personal and corporate life.
Similarly, an exclusive emphasis on orthopraxis often results
in disregard for essential doctrines that ground our faith and
from which just and righteous life must flow. Samuel Solivan, a
North American Hispanic theologian, has suggested that
"orthopathos" provides the necessary link between orthodoxy
and orthopraxis.[6] By considering the committed and deeply felt
response of the heart and will to the truth and its expression in
life, the Christian teacher can foster the connection being made
between orthodoxy and orthopraxis.

In addition to the explicit definitions of Coleman and Palmer,
one can define teaching in relation to an image or metaphor.

6. Samuel Solivan, "Orthopathos: Interlocutor between Orthodoxy and
Praxis," *Andover Newton Review* 1 (Winter 1990): 19–25.

One such image is suggested by Amy Lowell: "Teaching is like dropping ideas into the letter box of the human subconscious. You know when they are posted but you never know when they will be received or in what form."[7] This image suggests the risk involved in teaching and perhaps the place of serendipity and mystery. For me, an enduring image of teaching centers around the experience of being at table with Jesus and other disciples at the celebration of a meal, in particular the Lord's Supper. The image is that of a feast artfully served that welcomes all to participate, and it suggests the need for teaching to be an inviting and joyful celebration.[8]

In Christian teaching we recognize that the central table for our consideration is the Lord's table, which is also called Holy Communion or the Eucharist. As Holy Communion, this church sacrament or ordinance denotes the relationship initiated by God in Jesus Christ that welcomes all to partake of God's gracious offer. As Eucharist, this celebration denotes the participants' response of thanksgiving to such an offer that issues in a sense of fulfillment and joy. It is also significant that the Lord's Supper is the repeated sacrament or ordinance of the Christian church that denotes the need for continual nurture and relationship. This continual character of the sacrament, along with the character of being at table in general, is a fitting image for what is sought in the process of Christian teaching.

The power of being at table with the resurrected Jesus is described in Luke 24:28–35, where the disciples on the road to Emmaus experience joy with the opening of their eyes and of the Scriptures. The teacher they encountered as a stranger along the road was disclosed as their Lord and Savior in the breaking of bread together. But the Gospels also describe the experience of those who had not been welcome at the table. In Matthew 15:21–28, a Syro-Phoenician woman, one who been excluded,

7. Quoted by C. Roland Christensen, "Introduction," in *The Art and Craft of Teaching*, ed. Margaret Morganroth Gullette (Cambridge: Harvard University Press, 1982), xiv.

8. Allan Bloom uses this image in describing education as "putting the feast on the table." See *The Closing of the American Mind* (New York: Simon and Schuster, 1987), 51. In referring to Bloom I do not embrace Bloom's analysis of higher education or his perennialist philosophy. His work might be better entitled *The Challenge of Opening the Closed American Mind*.

confronts Jesus about the possibility of metaphorically sitting at table with him. Jesus recognized the faith of this Gentile woman, and her daughter was healed. Both the woman and her daughter were figuratively welcomed to partake of what Jesus was offering. It is noteworthy that the Pharisees and scribes were offended by Jesus' welcoming of sinners and by his eating with them during his ministry (Luke 15:2).

As a Christian teacher, one is conscious of those who may feel welcome at the table, as well as those who have been intentionally or unintentionally excluded from participation and therefore feel unwelcome. Like Jesus, the teacher must consider who needs to be invited to sit at table on equal terms with other guests. A teacher must also consider what will not only delight, but also nourish those at table. In addition, one is conscious of the mystery of community that is a gift of God. Yet the teacher must recognize that trust is needed to sit and partake together at table. A teacher can build that trust by allowing adequate time to foster open, supportive relationships.

Even with the best possible preparation for a meal, a host must allow for the unexpected and reserve space for the unexpected guest. In Jewish tradition the empty chair for Elijah at the passover meal recognizes this need. In Christian tradition Jesus is always the unseen guest at every table and teaching event. The responsibility of the teacher is to put as much as possible on the table. This requires disclosure of what often operates at the level of a hidden agenda or curriculum along with honest acknowledgment of areas not known by the teacher. This disclosure does not guarantee the response of participants-guests because the choice of receiving, ingesting, and embracing what is offered is that of those taught. This is an inherent risk in teaching that cannot be eliminated even with the most careful planning.

Being at table recognizes the importance of partnership, of community with a variety of persons that issues in an experience of joy, wonder, and awe in relationship with Jesus. It is this encounter with the resurrected Lord that Christian teachers are to nurture and to wait upon. This they do in their efforts to be at table with those to whom they have been called to teach. Being at table in teaching can be a profound experience of vulnerability, risk, hospitality, disclosure, pain, and joy. Nevertheless, teaching of this quality is worth our best efforts along with our conscious dependence upon God's grace and presence. Beyond my use of the table, a variety of other images or metaphors might be suggested to capture different dimensions of teaching, each of which can explore a unique facet of the art and craft of teaching.[9]

A View of Learning

As a psychological term, learning has generally been defined as a process by which behavior, or the potentiality for behavior, is modified as a result of experience. In a broader conception, I define learning as the process of change in one's knowledge, beliefs, values, attitudes, feelings, skills, or behaviors as a result of experience with the natural or supernatural environment. Nicholas P. Wolterstorff helpfully describes three types of learning that are of particular interest to the Christian educator who uses the broader definition:

1. *Cognitive learning*, which is acquiring a true belief about something
2. *Ability learning*, which is a capability, competence, or skill
3. *Tendency learning*, which is acquiring an inclination or disposition to act in certain ways in various types of situations[10]

Wolterstorff's classification is a welcome alternative to Benjamin Bloom's knowledge/affect/action taxonomy for learning. This alternative encourages viewing learning as a holistic achievement and one that has a direct impact upon life. Such an

9. For a discussion of metaphors in relation to curriculum that have direct implications for one's view of teaching see Robert W. Pazmiño, *Foundational Issues in Christian Education: An Introduction in Evangelical Perspective* (Grand Rapids: Baker, 1988), 210–14.

10. Nicholas P. Wolterstorff, *Educating for Responsible Action* (Grand Rapids: Eerdmans, 1980), 3–6. For a review of this work see Robert W. Pazmiño, Review of *Educating for Responsible Action*, in *TSF Bulletin* 6 (March–April 1983): 19–20.

alternative is consistent with a Christian understanding of learning that includes the aspect of response to God's truth.

In the Old Testament, learning (Heb.: *lamad*) referred to a process in which the understanding of God's law and will, and the experience of God's love issued in action and obedience corresponding to the law. Learning included an emphasis upon doing God's will in one's personal and corporate life.[11] This perspective complements the intended results of Christian teaching, namely, that the total lives of individuals will be transformed as a result of divine teaching. In the New Testament, learning is closely tied to the call to be a disciple of Jesus Christ. In this context, learning (Gk.: *manthano*) meant putting one's faith in Jesus Christ and following him in works of compassion and service.[12] Learning in the biblical sense implied a life of discipleship, service, and love of and obedience to God. In order to fulfill these obligations in learning, the New Testament believer had to rely upon the continuing work and filling of the Holy Spirit. Learning in the biblical sense called for a complete response of the person to God's teaching. Clearly, the initiative in this teaching/learning process is with the divine agent. At the heart of biblical education is God teaching God's creatures. But God's teaching implies a human response of either love, obedience, and life on the one hand, or indifference, disobedience, and death on the other hand. Physical as well as spiritual life or death is in view. In the case of the Christian teacher, student response may not entail the direct, immediate consequences of life or death, yet response is of great importance when the content is God's revealed truth and the truth is discovered or discerned in the world.

Both teaching and learning are high callings in the Christian sense. The methods that are chosen and perpetuated in Christian education must embody these understandings. The teacher who most exemplified these methods was Jesus Christ himself in his earthly ministry. Therefore, it is important to consider the example of the master teacher in his teaching methods.

11. Dietrich Muller, "Disciple, Follow, Imitate, After," in *The New International Dictionary of New Testament Theology*, ed. Colin Brown, 3 vols. (Grand Rapids: Zondervan, 1975), 1:484–86.

12. Ibid., 1:486–90.

Jesus' Teaching Methods

While recognizing the unique character of Jesus' redemptive mission on earth as God's anointed one, Christians can discern in Jesus' methodology a pattern for the task of making disciples. Jesus' teaching did focus upon the formation of the twelve apostles, along with a wider host of persons, including a number of women who along with John remained faithful at the foot of the cross. The formation of these disciples in a distinct first-century Palestinian context has significance for the ongoing task of making disciples, a task which was assigned to the followers of Jesus in the Great Commission (Matt. 28). The commission of Jesus to his followers stresses the task of making disciples as they go into all the world. This task involves inviting people into the Christian community and initiating them through their baptism. It also involves teaching the new disciple to obey all that Jesus himself taught his disciples, itself a lifelong undertaking. The results of Jesus' efforts cannot be assessed only by the response of persons prior to his death. His work was carried on by the twelve apostles and a host of other followers in the first-century church. One must also recognize the ministry of the Spirit of Christ begun at Pentecost and evaluate the effects of Jesus' teaching in the light of the resurrection. Throughout history, those who have considered this broader perspective have found much that is instructive in Jesus' methodology for the thought and practice of Christian education.[13] One of the scholars who has studied Jesus as a teacher, Donald Guthrie, observed that the crux of the issue about Jesus'

13. For classic works on Jesus as teacher, see A. B. Bruce, *The Training of the Twelve* (Grand Rapids: Kregel, 1971), originally published in 1894; Herman H. Horne, *Teaching Techniques of Jesus: How Jesus Taught* (Grand Rapids: Kregel, 1978), originally published in 1920 under the title *Jesus: The Master Teacher*; and Lewis J. Sherrill, *The Rise of Christian Education* (New York: Macmillan, 1944), 83–96. For more recent contributions see Matt Friedman, *The Master Plan of Teaching: Understanding and Applying the Teaching Styles of Jesus* (Wheaton: Victor, 1990); Joseph A. Grassi, *Teaching the Way: Jesus, the Early Church and Today* (Lanham, Md.: University Press of America, 1982), 25–68; Donald Guthrie, "Jesus," in *A History of Religious Educators*, ed. Elmer L. Towns (Grand Rapids: Baker, 1975), 15–38; and Marianne Sawicki, *The Gospel in History: Portrait of the Teaching Church, The Origins of Christian Education* (New York: Paulist, 1988), 41–68.

teaching approach lies with one's attitude to authority. He argues that Jesus' approach is timeless because truth carries its own authority, even in a time when authority is rejected. A lack of respect for the source of authority is not warranted in the case of Jesus and in the case of his teaching methods.[14] Thus, I conclude that a study of Jesus' teaching methodology is both warranted and fruitful.

In the New Testament Jesus is referred to approximately forty-five times as teacher, compared with approximately twenty times as savior. One possible implication of this fact is that Jesus' teaching ministry warrants attention in some proportion to the study of his ministry as savior. In considering Jesus' teaching methods, it is possible to identify both the general principles and their particular features. In relation to both these general principles and specific features, it is also possible to suggest some implications for the current practice of teaching.[15]

General Principles and Implications for Practice

JESUS' TEACHING WAS AUTHORITATIVE

Jesus taught as one who had authority (Mark 1:21–22). This authority was authenticated in terms of the content of his teaching and in terms of his person. The content of his teaching was the revelation of God, for he spoke with the words of God the Father (John 14:23–24). In addition, Jesus' life and ministry authenticated the authority of his teaching.

Implications: The Christian teacher's teaching is authoritative to the extent to which it is faithful to God's special and general revelation. Authority for the Christian teacher is derived and not inherent in his or her status, but inherent in the function of sharing God's words and in God's calling and anointing. The teacher's life and ministry must authenticate the truth of the teaching. The Christian teacher must choose methods that complement and support biblical content. Such a choice does not exclude variety and creativity. The Christian teacher must

14. Guthrie, "Jesus," in *A History of Religious Educators*, 37.
15. James S. Stewart outlines these areas in *The Life and Teachings of Jesus Christ* (Nashville: Abingdon, n.d.), 64–71.

also help students grapple with the implications of and the responses appropriate for this truth shared. The Christian teacher must strive not to have the methods subvert or contradict the goals and content of the teaching.

JESUS' TEACHING WAS NOT AUTHORITARIAN

While being authoritative, Jesus' teaching was not forced or imposed upon his hearers. A striking example of this principle is recorded in John 6:60–69:

> On hearing it, many of his disciples said, "This is a hard teaching. Who can accept it?"
> Aware that his disciples were grumbling about this, Jesus said to them, "Does this offend you? What if you see the Son of Man ascend to where he was before! The Spirit gives life; the flesh counts for nothing. The words I have spoken to you are spirit and they are life. Yet there are some of you who do not believe." For Jesus had known from the beginning which of them did not believe and who would betray him. He went on to say, "This is why I told you that no one can come to me unless the Father has enabled him."
> From this time many of his disciples turned back and no longer followed him.
> "You do not want to leave, too, do you?" Jesus asked the Twelve.
> Simon Peter answered him, "Lord, to whom shall we go? You have the words of eternal life. We believe and know that you are the Holy One of God."

What is the context of the response of these disciples? Jesus was teaching in the synagogue in Capernaum and was describing his ministry as offering the bread of life. His challenging teaching included the words in verses 54–56, which were hard to understand: "Whoever eats my flesh and drinks my blood has eternal life, and I will raise him up at the last day. For my flesh is real food and my blood is real drink. Whoever eats my flesh and drinks my blood remains in me, and I in him."

Jesus offered the truth of his hard teaching and allowed those who heard either to accept or to reject his words. Jesus trusted in the power of the truth he communicated to convince his disciples. He did not force compliance or impose his understanding

126

upon the will of his students. This does not suggest that Jesus avoided making clear and definite demands upon his followers. Rather, Jesus specified the costs and demands of discipleship and encouraged his followers to make personal commitments.

Another example of this principle is the account of Jesus' rejection in his hometown of Nazareth (Mark 6:1–6). Because Jesus did not force or impose his teaching upon others, he valued the response of his hearers and was affected by it. Jesus did no miracles except to heal a few sick people because of the lack of faith of his hearers in Nazareth. He was amazed at their disbelief and its consequences.

Implications: Christian teachers are called to provide freedom for their students to grapple with the truth and implications of their teachings. This can be done by posing questions and allowing for dialogue and interaction that focus on implications. It can also be done with the use of such methods as case studies and problem-solving tasks. This implication must be qualified in terms of the maturity and capabilities of the students involved. With youth and adults a greater level of freedom is possible as compared with preschool and school-age children. But even with children, allowing for limited choices and increased responsibilities can be an effective teaching strategy. In relation to methods, this second principle suggests the need for increased student participation and responsibilities if learning is to be applied and owned in life. In the light of Jesus' experiences, it also suggests a realistic awareness of the inherent risks of teaching, which include rejection.

JESUS' TEACHING ENCOURAGED PERSONS TO THINK

This third principle is illustrated in John 6:60–69. Jesus stimulated serious thought and questioning in his teaching and he expected his hearers to carefully consider their personal commitment to the truths he shared. In response to many inquiries, he did not supply simple, ready-made answers to every problem of life. Jesus expected his students to search their minds and hearts in relation to his teachings and to consider the realities of life. A further example is his frequent use of parables, which required various thought levels for his hearers to gain understanding. In encouraging others to think for themselves, Jesus posed questions and allowed for questioning.

Implications: Christian teachers need to be aware of the tendency to provide simple, ready-made answers for students who need to think for themselves. Teachers need to pose questions that require students to think about issues and real-life problems. The development of thinking skills needs to be considered at every level of education. Students need to be encouraged to discover truths through diligence in their study and reflection. Teachers can encourage creative thought as students make use of their curiosity in exploring various areas of study. These general methods require students to actively engage in their own education. Such a heightened level of thoughtful activity increases the possibility that students will appropriate the truths they studied and transfer their learning to new situations.

Jesus Lived What He Taught

Jesus incarnated his message faithfully in his life and ministry. Before commanding his disciples to serve and love one another as he had loved them (John 13:12–17, 34–35), Jesus demonstrated the full extent of his love by washing his disciples' feet. He then further demonstrated his love by laying down his life for his friends, his brothers, and his sisters (John 15:12–13).

Implications: Christian teachers are called to model those truths and qualities they hope to share with their students. They should seek to be and to become all that they affirm with their teaching. But likewise, Christian teachers must honestly compare their inconsistencies, contradictions, and sins with the sinless example of Jesus the Christ. Both concern for modeling and honesty regarding shortcomings imply the need for integrity in the lives of Christian teachers. Integrity can be defined as a wholeness of character. Such integrity is manifested in the style and manner of the teacher and through the methods displayed in teaching. In addition, integrity necessitates that the teacher on occasion admit a lack of knowledge, acknowledge mistakes, and ask for forgiveness. A teacher's message in a classroom or other setting must transcend that context to include all of her or his life.

JESUS HAD A LOVE FOR THOSE HE TAUGHT

This fifth principle, like the fourth, is well illustrated from the passages cited from the Gospel of John. It was Augustine, another great teacher, who said "one loving spirit sets another on fire," and that was one secret of Jesus' success as a teacher. Jesus loved his students, his disciples, in a way that indicated the deep longings of every heart for an intimate relationship. But this relationship of love with Jesus was also characterized by an equal concern for truth as it was communicated by the master teacher.

Implications: John T. Granrose, in commenting on teaching, identified basic and advanced teaching skills. The first advanced skill in teaching that he emphasizes is love and respect for the students.[16] Love is a challenge for teachers when an adversarial relationship exists with students in some institutional settings. Such a relationship can develop from a wide variety of factors, including the compulsory nature of much schooling. Teachers are called upon to fulfill various roles including that of an authority and a friend. The blending of these roles requires patience and sensitivity and a concerted effort to interact with students both in and out of the classroom and with heavy commitments of time and energy.

Specific Features and Implications for Practice

JESUS' TEACHING WAS ORAL INSTRUCTION

Jesus spoke to his disciples and hearers and his words were not communicated in written form during his earthly ministry. This feature is consistent with the oral tradition that characterized the Hebrew nation. Current educational practice maintains that an exclusive reliance upon oral instruction does not readily facilitate learning and that the method results in students retaining only about 10 percent of the material they hear. What made the difference in Jesus' teaching? Part of the answer must be related to the authority of Jesus' teaching, but other

16. John T. Granrose, "Conscious Teaching: Helping Graduate Assistants Develop Teaching Styles," in *New Directions for Teaching and Learning: Improving Teaching Styles,* edited by Kenneth E. Eble (San Francisco: Jossey-Bass, 1980), 29.

factors must be cited. Jesus' teaching had great effect and was remembered because of the truth it revealed. The truth significantly affected the lives of his students and transformed their understanding and their lives. The truth of Jesus' teaching was also supported by his life and ministry. Though Jesus' teaching was oral, it manifested an amazing variety of forms. Robert Stein, in his study of Jesus' teachings, records thirteen language forms that Jesus regularly used. In addition, Jesus made extensive use of parables, which make up about 35 percent of Jesus' teaching as recorded in the synoptic Gospels.[17]

Implications: Christian teachers are not limited to oral forms of instruction, but can use an array of methods and techniques. This does not relieve the teacher of the responsibility to improve the use of language and to add variety to her or his oral instruction. But in a media-oriented society, teachers must make constructive use of various media as well as challenge students to gain such skills as listening to the reading of literature.

JESUS' TEACHING ADDRESSED SPECIFIC EVENTS

The occasional nature of Jesus' teaching points out that it was largely unpremeditated and aimed at the particular circumstances. This type of teaching illustrates the biblical injunctions of Deuteronomy 6, where parents were admonished to teach God's commandments to their children. This was to be done when they sat at home, when they walked along the road, when they lay down, and when they got up. This type of teaching required sensitivity to teachable moments in the lives of children or students. The normal course of activities presented opportunities for teaching. These often occurred as an experience or a thought was shared, or were often precipitated by a question posed by children or students themselves. More often, such teaching involved the foresight and sensitivity of the teacher to pose a question or share an insight.

In the case of Jesus, though his teaching can be described as occasional, it was not limited in its applicability. Jesus dealt with urgent and immediate needs, but his teachings had definite universal significance.

17. Robert Stein, *The Method and Message of Jesus' Teaching* (Philadelphia: Westminster, 1978).

Implications: Though a good deal of teaching in modern western society occurs in formal settings, the Christian teacher needs to be sensitive to elements of serendipity that occur before, during, and after regularly scheduled class times. These occasions can often provide unique opportunities for ministry and the development of relationships. Parents have many more opportunities to model the occasional nature of teaching through the normal and special times of family life. This presents a challenge in the fast-paced and overscheduled agendas of much of contemporary life. Nevertheless, the fine art of developing sensitivity to occasional teaching can be revived and cultivated.

JESUS' TEACHING WAS CONTEXTUALIZED

Contextualization, a popular term in current theological discussions, refers to the application and adaptation of truth to specific contexts or situations and the emergence of truth from specific contexts. Jesus' teaching was adapted to his audience and often emerged from questions posed by his audience. He personalized his teaching by establishing points of contact with various persons and groups and by gaining their involvement. Jesus placed himself at the point of his hearers and started from there. He was sensitive to what they were able to receive. This did not involve a compromise of his message or of the demands of following him. Rather, Jesus sought to be understood and communicated effectively by contextualizing his teaching. One example often cited in this regard is Jesus' teaching of the Samaritan woman at the well (John 4). Jesus' point of contact is the water available at the well and the experience of thirst. He progressively responds to the woman and reveals her spiritual needs. The culminating truth he offers is his very person as Messiah. Jesus tailored his teaching to address this woman's needs in those areas where she needed instruction and, ultimately, transformation.

Implications: Christian teachers must contextualize their teaching to address the needs and understandings of those with whom they seek to communicate. This presents the challenge of getting to know one's students. Persons are complex, and their needs and understanding change over time. The students' world is an essential subject for the study of the teacher, and address-

131

ing the issues and problems with which students are grappling is a strategy for effective teaching. Christian feminism has pointed up the need for inclusive language as a form of contextualizing in our time. The challenge is to have women's experience be normative in a world that has historically emphasized male categories and experience.

JESUS USED FIGURATIVE ELEMENTS IN HIS TEACHING

Jesus used illustrations, epigrams, paradoxes, and parables. He was vivid, figurative, symbolic, and concrete in his teaching. All these elements helped persons see the truths he was proclaiming. They were also used so that some would not see,[18] a blessing or a curse for his hearers depending upon their response to Jesus' teaching.

Implications: It is important that teachers strive to be understood by their students through the use of figurative and other elements. Students need to hear and see what is being said or shared if there is to be any hope of learning. Although this fact is basic to communication and effective education, it must also be pointed out that teaching may not always strive for absolute clarity or closure. In the process of discovering answers and discerning new truths, students gain more than if ready-made answers are provided. It is in the process of study that students can more readily appropriate and own discovered insights. This approach assumes that there is adequate opportunity for further reflection and discussion under the guidance of an experienced teacher in evaluating the learning experience.

Principles about Teaching Methods

Building upon a glimpse of Jesus' teaching, seven principles can guide the choice of teaching methods:

1. Begin with a larger framework
2. Recognize the complexity of the classroom
3. Cultivate a conscious reliance on the Holy Spirit
4. Maintain a genuine concern for persons

18. Matthew 13:10–17 provides insight regarding Jesus' use of parables and the impact of this method in his teaching upon various hearers.

5. Share the tasks, goals, and objectives of teaching with the students
6. Share significant content
7. Relate teaching efforts to the larger social, political, and economic context

Begin with a larger framework. The question of teaching methods must be related to a larger framework of educational questions. Too often the methodological question of how one should teach is asked in isolation from a clear understanding of the questions of what and why one is teaching as well as from questions concerning when, where, and whom one is teaching. With a concern to be contemporary, some teachers readily adopt faddish new methods without considering the purposes and effects of teaching in general. The dangers in such a methodological preoccupation are evident in considering the long-term effects of teaching. Purpose and content can become secondary to using the newest method or approach.

In addition to the larger framework of questions, values become an important issue in relation to methods. Christian teachers at all levels of education and involvement need to ask themselves: Does our methodology support Christian or spiritual values? Do our methods complement and confirm the purposes and content of our teaching? The method or process can never be allowed to subvert the message, though the method often is the message in certain contexts. If the method is the exclusive message in every context, then the method limits the role of reason and intellectual grappling with the truth. An example of this distortion would be the exclusive promotion of one method, such as learning centers, to emphasize the discovery aspect of learning. An implicit principle in such an approach is that all truth is discovered by personal initiative and activity and that one may not be able to receive truth as proclaimed and received. Another example might be the ready use of gaming techniques without providing opportunities for adequate debriefing and subsequent discussion. A larger framework forces consideration of a variety of approaches, methods, and techniques with a clear understanding of purposes.

133

Recognize the complexity of the classroom. Michael J. Dunkin and Bruce J. Biddle suggest that it is possible to identify a host of variables that affect classroom teaching (fig. 5).

With presage, context, process, and product variables, there is a complexity that must be considered by the teacher. Dunkin and Biddle helpfully outline the natural dimension of physical factors and the human dimensions but do not discuss the spiritual or divine dimension of teaching—a variable that Christian teachers are aware of. D. Campbell Wyckoff maintains that Christian teachers must consider this additional dimension. The Holy Spirit is the determinative environmental presence in Christian education. The challenge for the Christian teacher is to create a climate in which the Spirit of God may work most fruitfully in the lives of persons in the church, home, and classroom.[19] The Christian teacher must consider how the lordship of Christ influences teaching and how the Word of God, living and written, becomes living and active in the lives of students.

Another implication of the complexity of the classroom is that in planning methods one must allow for serendipity: unconditioned as well as conditioned or anticipated responses. Teachers must be flexible on occasion and plan for, as well as allow for, options in methods. This complexity can lead to genuine humility and creativity in teaching that enriches the experiences of students.

Cultivate a conscious reliance upon the Holy Spirit. Recognition of the complexity of the classroom can lead a teacher to despair unless one acknowledges the availability of divine resources. The Holy Spirit is concerned with the dissemination of truth and the transformation of persons in conformity with the will of God. Conscious reliance upon the Holy Spirit through prayer and a daily filling in the life of the teacher makes a difference. Reliance upon the Spirit leads to a sense of wonder, awe, and reverence for the workings of God in the lives of the participants or students. It leads to a dependence upon prayer before, during, and after the actual teaching. It leads to an openness to revised agendas in response to the Spirit's promptings and to the teacher sharing her or his experiences in addition to the content

19. D. Campbell Wyckoff, *The Tasks of Christian Education* (Philadelphia: Westminster, 1955), 104.

Figure 5
Model for the Study of Teaching*

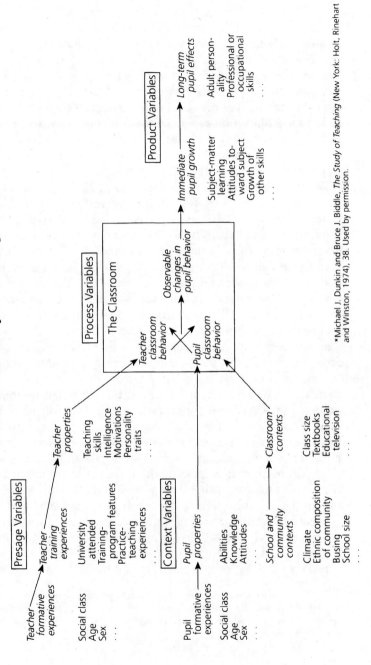

*Michael J. Dunkin and Bruce J. Biddle, *The Study of Teaching* (New York: Holt, Rinehart and Winston, 1974), 38. Used by permission.

of teaching. Such teaching can be described as "anointed" and results in a noticeable refreshment in teaching for both students and teacher.[20] The work of the Holy Spirit cannot be programmed or legislated in any way. The Spirit's work is not limited to teachers of unusual charisma as commonly understood, but every teacher has access to God's charisma or grace for the tasks of teaching. Jesus described to his disciples the role of the Holy Spirit in guiding them into all truth (John 16:13–15). The work of the Holy Spirit is a continued reality in the contemporary world, as it was in New Testament times.

Maintain a genuine concern for persons, both for others and for oneself as teacher. Teaching is an interpersonal affair. Whereas conservative Christians have stood for the truth, they have not always exemplified Christian love in concern for a diversity of persons. For example, evangelicals in the United States were not on the forefront of addressing issues of racism during the civil rights movement of the 1960s. Teachers of the Christian faith are called to consider seriously the participants in their teaching. This necessitates sensitivity to the felt and real needs of students, to their learning styles, and to appropriate responses at teachable moments in their lives. All of these areas are opportunities to demonstrate a love and concern beyond mere lip service and half-hearted commitments.

In addition to a concern for others, the Christian teacher is called to consider herself or himself. Part of that consideration involves a commitment to develop one's gifts and abilities to the fullest. To do this, teachers must have a sensitivity to their unique teaching style and to their strengths and weaknesses. Christian teachers need to share their lives as well as their doctrine, as did the apostle Paul. His words were: "We loved you so much that we were delighted to share with you not only the gospel of God but our lives as well, because you had become so dear to us" (1 Thess. 2:8). In his instructions to Timothy, Paul shared a similar message: "Set an example for the believers in speech, in life, in love, in purity," and "Watch your life and

20. Disappointment is inevitable in the actual practice of teaching. This is the risk of teaching. But some people may *not* be *teachers* called to a particular setting or group with whom they are currently working. Though anointed, they may not be properly placed.

136

doctrine closely. Persevere in them, because if you do, you will save both yourself and your hearers" (1 Tim. 4:12b, 16). Such a description of Paul's ministry and his injunctions to Timothy suggest that in this concern for people, Christian teaching takes on the character of a ministry directed to whole persons. Therefore, the teacher is called to maintain and express this concern. This calling of the teacher is described effectively in Robert K. Greenleaf's *Teacher as Servant*. Greenleaf portrays the sacrificial outpouring of one teacher's life for his students.[21]

Share the tasks, goals, and objectives of teaching with students. This general principle depends upon the age and maturity of the students. Students vary in their abilities to assume responsibilities for their own learning, but all students need to have a clear understanding of the tasks, goals, and objectives of the teaching. Students can better participate in learning if they can own the proposed tasks, goals, and objectives. An issue that emerges in considering this principle is the place of coercion or imposition in teaching. The work of Paulo Freire, a Brazilian educator, is helpful on this issue.

In *Pedagogy of the Oppressed,* Freire maintains that one can distinguish between banking education and problem-posing education or conscientization. Banking education involves the imposition of content or learning upon the students without adequate consideration of their persons. This banking education severely limits the freedom of students to think or actively participate in the process. His description caricatures traditional forms of education that are largely authoritarian and transmissive in nature.

The main transaction of banking education is the transferring of information from the teacher and depositing it in the students. This is prescriptive or directive teaching, which Freire describes in terms of ten characteristics:

1. The teacher teaches, the students are taught.
2. The teacher knows all, the students know nothing.
3. The teacher thinks, the students are thought about.
4. The teacher talks, the students listen meekly.
5. The teacher disciplines, the students are disciplined.

21. Robert K. Greenleaf, *Teacher as Servant* (New York: Paulist, 1979).

6. The teacher chooses, the students comply with the teacher's choice.
7. The teacher acts, the students have the illusion of acting.
8. The teacher selects the content, the students adapt to it.
9. The teacher imposes professional authority, the students lose their freedom.
10. The teacher is the subject, the students are mere objects.[22]

In contrast with banking education, Freire advocates conscientization or problem-posing education, which is to result in the liberation of persons. This form of education seeks to replace hierarchical patterns characteristic of teacher/student relationships with dialogue and interactions of shared responsibility. The student becomes an "educatee/educator" and the teacher becomes an "educator/educatee." These new terms reflect new responsibilities of participants beyond traditional expectations. One expectation is that the student will move from dependence upon the teacher to a more independent position that eventually supports an interdependent relationship with the teacher in inquiry and mutual learning.

A sequence of methods implied by Freire's thought includes the following:

1. A thorough search into the life situation of the students
2. The choice of themes for discussion from the life situation of the people
3. A graphic presentation of these themes as the basis for discussion
4. An open discussion by all concerned on the themes represented
5. A commitment to action on the part of both students and teacher as a result of the discussion[23]

22. Paulo Freire, *Pedagogy of the Oppressed*, trans. Myra Bergman Ramos (New York: Seabury, 1970), 59.
23. These implications are stated in John Elias, "Paulo Freire: Religious Educator," *Religious Education* 71 (January–February 1976): 40–56. See the discussion of lesson planning in chapter 4 of this text.

This sequence centers upon adults, but these methods can be adopted for children and youth at appropriate levels of responsibility. Freire's insights imply more than just sharing the tasks, goals, and objectives of teaching, but also the power, responsibilities, and actual process of teaching with students.[24] Freire's perspective deserves careful consideration by Christian educators conscious of the need to treat students as whole persons.

Share significant content. A concern for methods must complement a consideration of content, though a caveat applies in any educational situation that encourages a preoccupation with methods to the relative exclusion of content. Such a situation may be the result of rapid societal changes along with the constant assessment of trends by teachers and other educators. While this assessment aids teachers in being relevant and in applying their message to their audience, it can foster a loss of focus upon the truth to be communicated. This caveat assumes that there is truth or content that needs to be shared in teaching. It does not discount the place of discovery on the part of students, but affirms the place of the teacher with insights that can expand and enrich the understanding of students.

In relation to the fifth principle, stated earlier, this mention of content raises an important question: Is the transmission or proclamation of truth by the teacher inherently representative of banking education as Freire describes this term? In my opinion this is not the case. Teachers can share their knowledge, values, and skills so as to equip and empower their students. This same knowledge can be shared with the intent of dominating, manipulating, and controlling students. But the difference lies in the intent of the teacher and the extent to which students are allowed to explore alternatives, to dialogue with the teacher while considering the content, and to personally appropriate the truths shared.

James MacGregor Burns's discussion of leadership provides insights for this question of the teacher's method of sharing content. Such a discussion of leadership is appropriate in considering how the teacher leads or directs students. Burns

---

24. A further discussion of Freire's insights is found in Pazmiño, *Foundational Issues*, 68–72.

describes moral leadership as having three characteristics as they can be applied to education:

1. Teachers share content and have a relationship not only of power, but of mutual needs, aspirations, and values in relation to students.

2. Students have adequate knowledge of alternative teachers and programs and the capacity to choose among those alternatives without coercion or imposition, except for the coercion of truth itself.

3. Teachers take responsibility for their commitments.[25]

Thus it is possible to share content without succumbing to the limitations of banking education as described by Freire. This distinction in sharing content can be further explored by considering the differences between manipulation and influence. Every teacher should seek to influence students, but not to manipulate them. Manipulation in teaching implies deception, unawareness on the part of the students, inappropriate control, and distrust. By comparison, influence in teaching implies mutual knowledge, a freedom to disagree, no imposition of values, and a freedom to make personal decisions. Sharing content in this way was exemplified in the teaching ministry of Jesus as described earlier.

In sharing content, the teacher must consider the logical, psychological, and sociological order of the content. A logical order of content emerges from a rational, objective, or deductive division of the subject matter from the perspective of the academic discipline or area of study. The psychological order is that order assuming an intuitive, subjective, or inductive appropriation of the subject matter from the perspective of the students. The sociological order stresses the roles and responsibilities persons must assume in their community and society. In teaching, relative emphasis shifts among these three poles. For example, a course in systematic theology might emphasize the logical order of content by following an expo-

25. James MacGregor Burns, *Leadership* (New York: Harper and Row, 1978), 4–10.

sure to the doctrines of authority, of Scripture, of God, of persons, and eventually of end things. By comparison, a course in personal ethics might address such issues as racism, sexism, abortion, contraception, capital punishment, war, homosexuality, civil disobedience, and euthanasia in the order of concern to students. A course in practical theology might focus upon the various responsibilities of participants in such areas of ministry as worship leadership, counseling, or teaching.

Relate teaching to larger social, political, and economic context. The Christian gospel has implications for all of life and is concerned for whole persons. There is a danger in teaching so focused on local concerns, defined by the walls of the classroom, as to ignore the global situation. Another danger of particular significance for Christian educators is the danger of over-spiritualizing their teaching and ignoring the call to be in the world while not being of it. Christian teachers cannot be faithful to the gospel and isolate the classroom from the world. There is need for appropriate detachment in teaching for the purpose of reflection and study. But such detachment or coming apart for awhile assumes a corresponding commitment to engagement with the world as the focus of God's continuing activity and concern.

The challenge for the Christian teacher is, as Karl Barth has suggested, to read the newspaper along with the Bible and to see the world through the eyes of those less privileged and blessed. The tendency is to be so accustomed to western perspectives that one cannot appreciate the vast majority of humanity. The perspective of the world as a global village must be nurtured, and it is the responsibility of teachers to expose students to worlds beyond their imagination and immediate experience.

Richard H. deLone, in *Small Futures: Children, Inequality, and the Limits of Liberal Reform,* challenges teachers in the United States to dispel a cultural blindness to the significance of social structure and the dynamics of political and social structure in the lives of students, specifically children.[26] Teachers have generally been sensitive to the micro-environments of the

---

26. Richard H. deLone, *Small Futures: Children, Inequality, and the Limits of Liberal Reform* (New York: Harcourt Brace Jovanovich, 1979).

family, school, and community, without considering the impact of the wider society or macro-environment upon students. This wider environment must be considered if teaching is to be effectual. How can a teacher be expected to understand and assess the effects of the macro-environment? Teachers can explore how diverse social structures and systems might affect their students. In addition, they can be sensitive to personal and social histories as they provide insights for understanding the needs and sensitivities of their students. Such information can be gained by networking with agencies, centers, and schools that specialize in study, research, and communication.

The seven general principles for methods can aid the teacher in planning, implementation, and evaluation of teaching. These principles lead to an exploration of basic guidelines and specific factors in methodological decisions.

Basic Guidelines

Be flexible in planning methods, allowing for options and variability in the response of students. Teaching is a complex human activity, and for the teacher this implies that teaching itself is risky and often opportunistic. It is opportunistic in the sense that the teacher may respond to unexpected elements, and of variable student actions. This guideline does not negate the need for careful preparation and planning, but fosters openness to revise plans to meet educational needs revealed in each situation.

Be clear in presenting procedures and content. Clarity about procedure and subject matter facilitates learning. In addition, teachers need to be clear about their purposes, goals, values, and intentions. This additional clarity can include the negotiation of purposes and goals with the participants. Adult students also need to be clear about their purposes, goals, values, and intentions if any negotiation is to occur.

Be knowledgeable about one's students. A working knowledge of students' age, development, needs, expectations, and goals contributes to decisions about methods. A teacher needs to be aware of the diverse learning styles of members of her or his class. Knowledge of these styles along with the teacher's own teaching style can contribute to effectiveness in the classroom.

Contextualize: Know the situation. Jesus' teaching techniques varied with the context. He established a point of contact with the intent of being heard. Certain groups and cultures are socialized to learning by particular methods. On occasion, groups can be gradually exposed to new methods and techniques, but teachers must adapt their message to forms that can be appropriated by students in their context. Sensitivity to the time of the occasion must supplement an awareness of the place.

Recognize that there is no ideal method. Given this recognition, it is important that teachers know of and be competent in using a variety of methods. If the goal is for students to learn as well as possible, the teacher needs to provide opportunity for them to participate in learning. As Freire points out, there are two dangers in teaching. One danger is mere activism that emphasizes learning by doing without a corresponding concern for thought and reflection. The other danger is mere verbalism that stresses thought, reflection, and speech that are divorced from practical implications or the realities of life.[27] Both dangers are to be avoided.

Depend upon God and the ministry of the Holy Spirit. A Christian world view embodies the joint and cooperative efforts of divine and human agents. In an ultimate sense, God is the teacher of persons as God's creatures, and in the educational process, the special ministry of the Holy Spirit is applying God's truths to the hearts and minds of persons. In a proximate sense, persons cooperate with God in teaching, guiding, and sharing with other persons about God and the multidimensional aspects of creation. This cooperative effort is not devoid of conflict, inconsistencies, and tensions, but holds great potential for renewal in human life.

In addition to these basic guidelines, some specific factors influence the choice of a method:

a. The goals and objectives of the particular lesson in relationship to a unit or course of study (students need to be aware of points of continuity and discontinuity with previously studied material)

---

27. Freire, *Pedagogy*, 75–76.

    b. Specific characteristics of learners, including their age, abilities, education, and unique needs
    c. The content of the lesson
    d. Available human material resources
    e. The allotted time

Additional factors can be named, but these serve to outline those elements that are considered either explicitly or implicitly in deciding how to teach within a particular context.

In conclusion, Christian educators can draw norms and implications about educational methods from the model of Jesus' teaching. General principles and basic guidelines support the insight that teaching is more of an art or a craft than a precise science. This situation calls for the creative response of Christians who are receptive to the continuing work of the Holy Spirit in the lives of teachers and learners alike. Receptivity to the Holy Spirit includes an openness to educational evaluation, which is the topic of chapter 6.

6

Educational Evaluation

Evaluation, either explicit or implicit, is essential to most human activities. Reflection upon action is crucial to assess its effectiveness and to provide insights for future action. Educational evaluation involves the question of values and in the case of Christian education, Christian values. One can rewrite the word *evaluation* to highlight this reality: e-*value*-ation. Before considering the specifics of educational evaluation, Christian educators must wrestle with the question of values in education.

The Question of Values

Values are generally described as concepts to which worth, interest, and goodness have been attributed. Values are choices of concern which by their nature embody theological considerations for the Christian. They deal with what is desirable, meaningful, enduring, and therefore worthy of passing on to succeeding generations through teaching. In education values help to identify those goals, ideals, and ultimate ends of thought and action that make up the fabric of life and therefore of educational content. Values also identify what should be the focus in educational planning, practice, and evaluation. As the *Taxonomy of Educational Objectives* suggests, values inherently involve belief in propositions, belief in the desirability of those propositions, and a commitment to them that calls for personal conviction and full involvement.[1] To educate is to teach at every point the complex web of religious, moral, and intellectual values that define the character of any community and society.[2]

In *Foundational Issues in Christian Education,* I set out the fourfold obligations of Christians in relation to education: Christians must personally own and live the values they profess within the educational content and context; Christians must translate their values into specific purposes and goals to be accomplished in educational programs and considered in evaluation; Christians need to pursue their values in the educational structures in which they are called to participate and serve; and Christians must be open to the continual process of conversion or renewal in reaffirming essential values that may have been forgotten.[3] These four obligations impinge upon the explicit, hidden, and null curricula (chap. 4).

First, Christian values need to be explicit in relation to the stated purposes, goals, and content of Christian education so as to enable the integration of any subject matter with the Christian faith. Second, Christian values need to be embodied in the hidden or implicit curriculum in terms of the modeling of Christian character, relationships, and the unique quality of Christian community that balances love, truth, and other Christian virtues. Third, Christian values need to be prominent in discerning the nature of the null curriculum with an openness to reaffirm those perspectives, procedures, and processes that have been left out, but that are essential for renewal in Christian education. For example, the Christian value or virtue of "speaking the truth in love" may be forgotten not only in the explicit

1. David R. Krathwohl, Benjamin S. Bloom, and Bertram B. Masia, *Taxonomy of Educational Objectives, Handbook II: Affective Domain* (New York: David McKay, 1964), 176–85.

2. For a fuller discussion of the place of values and axiology, which is the study of values, see Robert W. Pazmiño, *Foundational Issues in Christian Education: An Introduction in Evangelical Perspective* (Grand Rapids: Baker, 1988), 91–96, 214–17.

3. Also see John W. Gardner, "Engagement of Values in Public Life," *Harvard Divinity Bulletin* (October–November 1984): 5–6.

curriculum, but also in the hidden curriculum. The tendency in some educational settings is to speak the truth without nurturing loving relationships that consider the students' readiness to discern and receive that truth as an important part of the hidden curriculum. A tendency in other educational settings is to so stress love and supportive relationships that little or no opportunity is provided to discern and confront the truth in the explicit curriculum.

The question of values also impinges upon the evaluation of educational methods. Individual differences and distinct teaching styles must be recognized, but the definitions of teaching offered by both Lucien E. Coleman and Parker J. Palmer suggest that teachers can be evaluated in terms of both appropriate activity and receptivity in the choice and use of methods.[4] In terms of my metaphor of a table artfully prepared, the implied values are those of hospitality, variety, and joy. These values translate into the consideration of classroom climate, the extent of choice in teaching methods, and the enjoyment experienced by both teachers and students. All of these factors can be assessed in evaluation. In addition, both the seven principles and the six basic guidelines (chap. 5) incarnate values modeled in the teaching ministry of Jesus, and these principles are appropriate for evaluating the effectiveness and results of teaching and learning in contemporary contexts.

Christian educators must also raise the question of values in considering educational structures. By raising such a question, educators are forced to see the bigger picture and to move from parochial to societal and global concerns. Educators must assess the extent to which they have recognized the connections across the structures and the extent to which they have fostered the transfer of learning from their setting to other settings. In the process of evaluation, one must ask if the students can integrate learning with life, if the teacher can see individual students and groups of students in relation to their contexts, and if persons are prepared for their public, corporate, and communal life. The school or church must see itself as a particular public that is in some ways both representative of and an alternative to the wider public. In evaluation, the challenge is to assess the

4. Coleman's and Palmer's definitions are discussed in chapter 5.

extent to which a particular educational setting has culturally accommodated in both appropriate and inappropriate ways in relation to Christian values. For example, the wider culture in the United States stresses that the worth of individuals depends upon the abundance of their material possessions. How is this value affirmed or critiqued within a particular Christian education setting? This is an important question for evaluation. Similarly, in the United States the wider culture has tended to stress the importance of individuals at the expense of a concern for community. How does a Christian world view compare with this value of individualism? Another question that particularly affects educational evaluation is the place of objectives that have been a dominant cultural emphasis in the United States.

The Place of Educational Objectives: Affirmation and Critique

Clarity with regard to behavioral, problem-solving, and expressive objectives assists in the process of evaluation, for the processes and results of teaching and learning differ with each of these distinct ends or goals. It seems that one could anticipate precision in teaching itself and in evaluation of behavioral objectives. But this assumption must be questioned.

A behavioral or instructional objective can be defined as a "statement which describes what students will be able to do after completing a prescribed unit of instruction."[5] By stating what students will be able to do, teachers can assess or measure whether students can in fact do what was intended after the prescribed instruction. By such assessment or measurement, typically accomplished through some sort of testing, teachers can evaluate the effectiveness of their teaching in terms of student learning.

What can be affirmed in such an approach to teaching, learning, and evaluation? First, behavioral objectives can help focus efforts in teaching and learning by providing specificity. It is popularly stated that if you aim at nothing in particular, that is what you will accomplish—nothing. Second, behavioral objectives provide for order and for the progressive introduction of

5. Donald L. Griggs, *Teaching Teachers to Teach: A Basic Manual for Church Teachers* (Nashville: Abingdon, 1974), 12.

new materials consistent with students' capacities. Third, a clear statement of objectives facilitates the design and evaluation of teaching by making intentions explicit. Fourth, behavioral objectives provide a practical means by which to evaluate the effectiveness of teaching through the identification of observable benchmarks. Students have a greater sense of both accountability and achievement with such benchmarks and can evaluate their own learning. Fifth, setting behavioral objectives can foster the transfer of learning by stating areas for change in students' behaviors, capacities, and thoughts. Sixth, the use of behavioral objectives can assist in providing adequate repetition for learning while avoiding redundancy. Seventh, the stating of behavioral objectives encourages clear communication of expectations by teachers to students so that students can more readily become active participants in the teaching-learning process.

Lawrence Stenhouse listed a number of criticisms of the use of behavioral objectives in educational evaluation. First, trivial learning behaviors are the easiest to state, and hence uses of objectives underemphasize the important outcomes of education. Second, the prescription of explicit objectives prevents the teacher from taking advantage of unexpected instructional opportunities. This results in a tyranny of objectives in teaching and evaluating. Third, measurability in behavioral objectives implies behavior that can be objectively and mechanistically assessed. This expects too little from teaching and learning. In certain areas of life it is difficult to identify measurable student behaviors, such as in the fine arts, the humanities, and religion. Fourth, teachers rarely specify their goals in terms of measurable student behaviors. Fifth, measurability implies accountability in too narrow terms. Teachers are evaluated on their ability to produce results in learners rather than on the many bases used in general practice as indices of competence. Sixth, objectives are difficult and time-consuming to write and not worth the effort in teaching. Seventh, in evaluating the worth of teaching, the unanticipated results often are really important and deserve attention as compared with the intended results specified in behavioral objectives.[6] Stenhouse's criticisms provide

6. Lawrence Stenhouse, *An Introduction to Curriculum Research and Development* (New York: Holmes and Meier, 1975), 72ff.

149

necessary warnings for those who would rely exclusively upon behavioral objectives in the planning, practice, and evaluation of teaching. These criticisms point up the problems with exclusive dependence upon a production metaphor for teaching and curriculum.[7]

What possible conclusions can be drawn for educational evaluation from the discussion of the strengths and weaknesses of behavioral objectives? One conclusion lies in a distinction that can be made between training and education. According to Mauritz Johnson, training implies learning for use in predictable situations where teachers can anticipate and state behavioral objectives for students to accomplish in their learning. Learning in this case is replicative and applicable across settings. Education, in contrast with training, implies learning for use in unpredictable situations. Learning in this case is associative and interpretive, and its transfer to other settings requires different sensitivities and skills.[8] In education teachers are more prone to use problem-solving and expressive objectives. Elliot Eisner does not distinguish training from education in the stark terms Johnson proposes, but distinguishes two concerns in education and therefore in its evaluation. One concern is giving mastery of the knowledge and cultural tools already available, the essentials or fundaments of the faith in Christian categories. This first concern equates with Johnson's description of training (the predictable character of some learning that can be conceived in terms of behavioral objectives). A second concern in education is making possible creative responses that go beyond what is available and that help persons to develop and individualize it.[9] This second concern equates with Johnson's description of education (the unpredictable character of forms of learning that cannot be conceived in terms of behavioral objectives). To impose behavioral objectives upon this second concern is to limit the full potential of education and to narrowly define the task of educational evaluation.

7. See my discussion of this and other metaphors in *Foundational Issues*, 210–14.

8. Mauritz Johnson, "Definitions and Models in Curriculum Theory," *Educational Theory* 17 (April 1967): 127–40.

9. Elliot W. Eisner, *The Educational Imagination: On the Design and Evaluation of School Programs*, 2d ed. (New York: Macmillan, 1985), 119–20.

What then is recommended is an evaluative perspective that encompasses the three distinct types of objectives that are described in chapter 4: behavioral, problem-solving, and expressive. This perspective encourages the assessment of both predictable and unpredictable results of education and encourages accountability for both intended and unintended results of teaching. Thus, what is recommended for Christian educators is to move beyond a narrow and exclusive focus upon behavioral objectives in educational evaluation. What can be suggested for such a broader focus in educational evaluation that is not limited to the narrow accountability suggested by using behavioral objectives?

What Can Be Evaluated?

In addition to the general suggestions already given, Christian educators must grapple with the specifics of educational evaluation. In exploring the specifics, educators have distinguished formative evaluation from summative evaluation.[10] In formative evaluation the process of education is assessed. Questions about the explicit curriculum include: How do we improve the process? How are the stated purposes, goals, and objectives reached in the teaching and learning? How is the content introduced and appropriated? How are persons involved in the process? How is the educational content applied to the personal and corporate lives of the students, or how is the content transferred to settings beyond the teaching-learning situation itself? How are students engaged actively and receptively in the

10. For a more detailed discussion of evaluation in general education see C. M. Lindvall, *Measuring Pupil Achievement and Aptitude* (New York: Harcourt, Brace and World, 1967), and Arno A. Bellack and Herbert M. Kliebard, eds., *Curriculum and Evaluation* (Berkeley: McCutchan, 1977). For a more detailed discussion of evaluation in Christian education see Helen F. Spaulding, ed., *Evaluation and Christian Education: Discussion of Some Theological, Educational and Practical Issues* (New York: National Council of Churches in the U.S.A., Office of Publication and Duplication, 1960); D. Campbell Wyckoff, *How to Evaluate Your Christian Education Program* (Philadelphia: Westminster, 1962); C. Ellis Nelson, *Using Evaluation in Theological Education* (Nashville: Discipleship Resources, 1975); and Lowell E. Brown, *Sunday School Standards: A Guide for Measuring and Achieving Sunday School Success* (Glendale, Calif.: Gospel Light, 1981).

process? How is culmination or closure of the educational experience achieved?

In addition to these questions, others might be proposed in considering the hidden curriculum. In relation to the implicit components of the curriculum it would be appropriate to ask: What kind of relationships are being fostered between students and teachers in the process? How does the structure of the classroom foster or hinder the educational process? What kind of organizational pattern is being maintained, and how does this reflect or counteract the patterns that persist in the larger social system? How are values being communicated through the educational process and are these values appropriate? What processes of socialization and enculturation are operative in the educational experience, and can alternatives be suggested? What wider societal or communal functions are being served through the educational process that is being supported explicitly or implicitly?[11] Other questions emerge from a consideration of the sociology of education and include five named by John Eggleston:

1. What have been regarded as the essential knowledge, understanding, values, attitudes, and skills in the educational process (the elements of education)?
2. How have these elements been ranked in importance and status?
3. On what principles have these educational elements been distributed in the educational process? To whom and at what times has the education been made available and from whom has it been withheld?
4. What is the identity of the persons or groups whose definitions and decisions have prevailed in these matters?
5. Is it legitimate for these persons or groups to act in these ways?[12]

11. These questions emerge from Elizabeth Vallance's description of the hidden curriculum. See "Hiding the Hidden Curriculum: An Interpretation of the Language of Justification in Nineteenth-Century Educational Reform," *Curriculum Theory Network* 4 (1973–1974): 5–21.

12. John Eggleston, *The Sociology of the School Curriculum* (London: Routledge and Kegan Paul, 1977), 23.

Eggleston's questions serve to connect aspects of the explicit and implicit curricula by posing questions that are often not raised.

As might be anticipated, additional questions can be posed in relation to the null curriculum that are suggested both by Maria Harris's description of this curriculum and the five-task model, which has been proposed as a foundational form. These questions include the following: What options, alternatives, and perspectives have been eliminated from consideration in the educational process? What content, themes, and point of view have been left out? Why? What procedures have been left unused, such as the arts, play, and critical analysis? What educational processes, such as two-way dialogue, extensive consultation with participants, and active participation by students in decisions, have formed the null curriculum?[13] In addition, which of the connections in the five-task model have not been considered in the educational process of either the explicit or implicit curriculum? Not all of these questions would be posed in relation to each lesson, but could be posed in relation to the educational diet over time. This is crucial if teaching is to be a well-prepared table and provides a balanced diet for those invited to participate.

In contrast, summative evaluation assesses the results or products of education. An interest in products does not assume the exclusive emphasis on a productive metaphor for teaching, but an appropriate concern for discerning the fruits of teaching and learning. Summative evaluation includes the estimation of merit, worth, and value in relation to the broad purposes and goals of education. It considers the basic question "So what?" But it maintains an interest in discerning ultimate and penultimate concerns. Ultimate concerns for the Christian community include the purpose of glorifying and enjoying God forever, and penultimate concerns can include the five tasks of proclamation, community, service, advocacy, and worship.

In summative evaluation the results or products are assessed by answering the following questions: What are students able to do as a result of the instruction or training? How is this different

13. Maria Harris, *Fashion Me a People: Curriculum in the Church* (Louisville: Westminster/John Knox, 1989), 69.

from what students came into the class able to do? What specific knowledge, understanding, appreciation, attitudes, values, skills, and sensibilities do students demonstrate as a result of the teaching and learning? Is there significantly better student performance as a result of the teaching and learning that was experienced? Summative evaluation focuses upon the terminal, overall, or outcome results of education and in practice recognizes the value of independent input that provides an outside vantage point for assessment. In the United States this has resulted in a preoccupation with standardized objective testing on a broad national scale in public education. Christian education generally does not emphasize standardized testing.

Educators have tended to evaluate teaching in terms of a process, and learning in terms of products. The work of Thomas F. Green in *The Activities of Teaching* helps in exploring this distinction, which makes a difference for the type of evaluation possible. Green differentiates task from achievement in education. A task centers on a process, whereas an achievement centers on a product. To look is a process, but to find or to fail to find is an achievement. To treat an illness medically is a task, but to cure or to fail to cure is an achievement. To race or play is a task, but to win or lose is an achievement. To travel is a task, but to arrive (or complete a journey) or to fail to arrive is an achievement. Similarly, Green contends that to teach is a task, but to learn or to fail to learn is an achievement. Therefore, teaching *cannot* be understood as the kind of activity that causes learning, because it can occur when learning does not. Moreover, learning can occur when there is no teaching. Learning is sometimes a result of teaching, but it is neither causal nor a logical result. Teaching does not ignore products, but it is primarily a process to foster the realization of certain products.[14] Thus the evaluation of teaching should primarily focus on its character as a process and a task and only secondarily on the products or achievement of learning by students who may or may not engage in the process intended to foster their learning.

In evaluating the process of teaching, Joel Davitz, an educational psychologist, identified eight skills of teaching that can be

14. Thomas F. Green, *The Activities of Teaching* (New York: McGraw-Hill, 1971), 137.

subject to evaluation.[15] These teaching skills are associated with student learning. Because these skills can be learned and practiced by teachers, they can be evaluated in the process of education. The first skill is clarity of communication. Teachers must communicate clearly in both the subject matter and procedure. Clarity in subject matter refers to staying on the subject, being repetitive enough to allow for retention, following a sequence, and providing clear explanations. Procedural clarity refers to making explicit the goals of the process and how the students are expected to learn them.

The second skill is flexibility and the capability of using a variety of teaching methods. An effective teacher has a repertoire of methods, recognizing that all methods are good but must be used selectively. The effective teacher is able to decide which methods are appropriate for a particular learning task and group. A variety of teaching methods helps to maintain the interest of students, who have a variety of learning styles (chap. 4). A variety of learning styles implies that students will have different entry points for dealing with the educational content.

The third skill which can be evaluated and nurtured is enthusiasm. The enthusiastic teacher elicits the most learning, but this must be a focused enthusiasm that centers on the educational process and not on diversions. Student activation is related to learning and enthusiasm serves to activate students. Teachers can be excited about the teaching process itself, the tasks associated with learning, and the content and/or the interaction of teaching. Augustine said that one loving spirit sets another spirit on fire, and genuine enthusiasm can help ignite that fire.

A fourth skill is the maintenance of a task orientation in teaching. Effective teachers are able to keep students focused on the tasks of learning. Students can have fun in many appropriate ways, and some socializing is appropriate, but the job of learning must be engaged with the best possible effort, energy, and concentration. This is popularly described as keeping the

15. Joel R. Davitz (lecture presented at Teachers College, Columbia University, New York, New York, 25 April 1979). Davitz helpfully summarized insights gained from research on teaching in his lecture, and I have drawn from his work and elaborated on it in what follows.

students' "nose[s] to the grindstone" in order to accomplish the necessary learning tasks.

The ability to involve students in the teaching-learning process is a fifth skill. Students need to be hooked into learning intellectually, psychologically, and, where appropriate, physically. Cognitive activity is more important than motor activity, and adequate time on the learning tasks is required for students to gain from their participation. This skill for teaching and the corresponding area for evaluation does not equate with a stress only on learning by doing. Both action and reflection are needed for students to learn and to retain what they learn.

A sixth skill for teaching and subsequent evaluation is that of varying the level of discourse. Discourse can be at the level of facts, explanation, evaluative judgments, justification, critical analysis and synthesis, concrete realities, and abstract possibilities. Moving back and forth across these levels is important for effective learning. This movement helps to connect the learning with life and to creatively explore new possibilities with students. When the teacher varies the level of discourse, students are called upon to engage and appropriate the content in greater depth.

Davitz named the appropriate use of praise and criticism as a seventh skill contributing to learning and subject to evaluation. As with enthusiasm, praise and criticism must be both appropriate and genuine to be effective in facilitating learning. Teachers need to criticize preformance, not the student as a person. A moderate amount of praise is effective, but if it is inappropriate, distrust will be promoted between the students and teacher.

An eighth teaching skill that can be learned and practiced and is therefore subject to evaluation is a "metaskill." A metaskill is one that transcends the other skills and is viewed on a distinct level deserving greater attention. This metaskill is a capacity for self-analysis or self-evaluation. The effective teacher is capable of pursuing continuous self-study and analysis so that skills can be continually enhanced over time. Self-analysis includes openness and ability to receive the constructive criticism of others. But in the ministry of teaching one must anticipate the real cost of dealing with unwarranted criticism. By raising matters that center upon the ministry of teaching and the costs that Christians might be called be bear, Christian educators must decide by a comparison of Christian and cultural values, what are their commitments.

Christian Values and Cultural Values

The Christian faith calls for those who embrace it to evaluate their intentions, motives, and efforts in relation to Christian values. This evaluation must take place in a particular cultural context with its own values and ideals; these values may confirm, complement, or contradict Christian values.[16] The evaluation of intentions and motives can be explored in relation to a discussion of the interests, passions, and loves of education. These interests, passions, and loves in turn can be described as a spirituality of education.

Spirituality has to do with the knowledge and experience of God, which Christians affirm in relation to Jesus the Christ. But in a more general sense all people have some sort of spirituality because every person has what Augustine called an *ordo amoris,* an order of loves. Our spirituality is not what we explicitly express, nor what we profess to believe, but how we order our loves in life. That ordering may be implicit or explicit, but the resultant spirituality pervades our whole life and person.[17] The order of our loves is revealed through teaching and is therefore subject to evaluation.

By living, being, and teaching in a particular culture, teachers and students are immersed in social patterns and structures that connect education with distinct interests and passions. The work of Parker J. Palmer in exploring a spirituality of education identifies the connections between education or the acquisition of knowledge and various human interests, passions, or loves. Palmer names three distinct human interests that can

16. Lawrence A. Cremin makes use of the three terms *confirm, complement* and *contradict* in referring to different institutions or structures that educate (chap. 3). These terms can also relate to the relationship of distinct value orientations. See Lawrence A. Cremin, *Traditions of American Education* (New York: Basic, 1977), 128.

17. *Spiritual Formation in Theological Education: An Invitation to Participate* (Geneva, Switzerland: Programme on Theological Education, World Council of Churches, 1987), 8.

be associated with different conceptions and practices of education. Each of these interests fosters a distinct corporate spirituality, which remains implicit in the vast majority of teaching settings. The three interests are control, curiosity, and compassion. The student seeks, through applied empirical and analytical study, to gain control over a body of knowledge. This is the dominant cultural preoccupation or passion in a highly technical society like the United States. The knowledge gained through speculative, historical, and hermeneutical study seeks to discover knowledge as an end in itself, to satisfy curiosity. This is the dominant cultural passion that emerged from the Greek educational heritage and is affirmed in more traditional, classical, and liberal arts traditions. The knowledge that liberates is one that Palmer finds described in 1 Corinthians 8:1–3: "Now concerning food sacrificed to idols: we know that 'all of us possess knowledge.' Knowledge puffs up, but love builds up. Anyone who claims to know something does not yet have the necessary knowledge; but anyone who loves God is known by [God]" (NRSV). This knowledge is one associated with compassion or love.[18]

In such an analysis one is able to relate a personal order of loves (spirituality) and societal or communal interests with the honoring of knowledge or educational content. This analysis brings us back to consider the educational trinity (content, persons, and context) with an evaluation of the abiding spirituality that exists across these elements. One constant danger in accommodating to cultural values is the reductionism that can result. This reductionism can be illustrated by referring to the proposed educational trinity. All three of the elements need to be connected and embraced in a balanced way. In emphasizing any one or two of these elements to the exclusion of others,[19] six potential reductionist dangers are generated. The result can

18. Parker J. Palmer, *To Know as We Are Known: A Spirituality of Education* (San Francisco: Harper and Row, 1983), 6–10. Also see Jurgen Habermas, *Knowledge and Human Interests* (Boston: Beacon, 1971).

19. The work of Rolando Soto highlights this reductionism. See F. Ross Kinsler, "Kairos en la educación teológica: Un cambio de perspectiva desde abajo," *Vida y Pensamiento* 8 (Diciembre 1988): 22–24.

be a spirituality that is not holistic and is therefore questionable from a Christian perspective.

First, just emphasizing content can result in a traditionalism that fails to recognize the important contextual factors and the distinct needs of persons. Often traditions themselves emerged from a perspective that originally sought to acknowledge the context and persons involved. If this traditionalism focuses on the content of the Bible alone, a biblicism results that fails to adequately struggle with the need to interpret Scripture and the need to contextualize biblical truth in addressing modern situations. This criticism does not deny the legitimate place of continuity with the biblical world, but points up the corresponding need to recognize the place of change or discontinuity operating in persons and the wider communal and societal context.

Second, by emphasizing just the context of the community, society, or culture a reductionism results that can be named behaviorism, radicalism, or contextualism. This reductionism is so engaged with contextual issues and either the maintenance of cultural norms or their complete transformation that no adequate place is given to the individual needs of persons or the character of the content, which itself can be formative for the context. In the case of behaviorism the stress is upon fitting persons into existing or proposed cultural norms with a concern for conformity and careful shaping. In radicalism, the stress is upon opening up society to new possibilities, but with a definite agenda that does not often recognize individual differences.

Third, by emphasizing just persons and their individual experience and practice a reductionism results that can be named activism, personalism, or individualism. The stress upon personal perspectives, introspection, and actions that flow from self-awareness can result in preoccupation that fails to consider corporate realities and the place of content which can contribute the voices of tradition and the past that are essential to understanding personal reality and the possibilities for constructive action.

Fourth, the combination of interest in content and context is affirmed as compared with either traditionalism or radicalism. But this combination, which fails to recognize the place

159

of persons in the mix, results in the reductionism of intellectualism or verbalism. Intellectualism can connect the content to the context, understood as the society and culture, but fails to address the personal experience and practical issues that are confronted. The preferred stance in this perspective is theorizing and intellectual inquiry. But such a stance fails to consider the personal and practical consequences of what is discovered or conceived. This reductionism could be described as promoting abstract educational theory with applied theory suggesting personal and practical consequences.

Fifth, the combination of contextual and personal interests can be a welcome alternative to either radicalism or activism, but it too is subject to its own reductionism in failing to adequately consider the place of content or the inherited traditions. This reductionism can be named humanism, presentism, or contextualism, which in Christian tradition fails to allow for the place of Scripture, theology, and the insights gained from church history for addressing the problems of persons or the society. The neglect of the Christian heritage results in the loss of a sense of identity.

Sixth, the combination of interest in content and persons represents an improved alternative to the excesses of either traditionalism or activism. But it too, like the other less-than-complete combinations, fails to address the whole and ignores the essential place of the context, of the society and culture in which persons receive and grapple with the content. This reductionism is a literalism that seeks to make the personal application of content without critically understanding the wider communal and social context in which those persons live, move, and have their being shaped and defined.

Emphasizing one or two elements or poles to the exclusion of others creates imbalance and distortion. All the elements of content, persons, and context must be addressed to develop a critical perspective or a constructive and holistic approach to Christian education. This holistic approach is essential to the Christian gospel. It embodies Christian values as an alternative to accommodating to cultural and subcultural values, which too often result in the six reductionistic stances just named. As has been suggested, reductionism of any kind can make idols

160

of half truths and result in fragmentation. The guidelines that emerge from this analysis are the following: Do not sacrifice content at the expense of persons and/or the context; do not sacrifice persons at the expense of content and/or the context; and do not sacrifice the context at the expense of the content and/or persons in Christian education. A combinationist or ecological approach is being advocated in this work. This approach connects and blends, with critical discernment, the three elements of content, persons, and context. It has been argued that this approach is faithful to Christian values while it avoids the ever-present reductionism supported by various cultural values. But it too must be subject to continual evaluation and to the process of always being reformed in avoiding current and future reductionism.

Two additional considerations can be named in relation to the possible conflict between Christian and cultural values. One consideration is the existence of "morphological fundamentalism." Morphological fundamentalism refers to the tendency of churches, schools, and other educational structures to view their patterns or forms of life, including educational forms, as God-given, eternal, and beyond question.[20] Such a view limits the possibility for critical evaluation and for exploring constructive alternatives. To counter morphological fundamentalism, which can result in the protection of idolatries in educational ministries, educators are called to embrace a Reformation or Protestant principle that the theologian Paul Tillich named.[21] Tillich observed that it is the nature of institutions and ministries to be formed on the basis of a powerful new insight or demand. Gradually the form of the institution will take over the function and become an end in itself. Institutions and ministries lose sight of their purpose and become self-perpetuating. The Protestant principle is an explicit awareness of this tendency and a continual reminder to guard and act against this tendency and

20. See J. C. Hoekendijk and Hans Schmidt, "Morphological Fundamentalism," in *Planning for Mission: Working Papers on the New Quest for Missionary Communities*, ed. Thomas Weiser (New York: U.S. Conference for the World Council of Churches, 1966), 134–37.

21. Paul Tillich, *The Protestant Era*, trans. James L. Adams (Chicago: University of Chicago Press, 1948), 161–81.

process. This Protestant principle is important to affirm in the process of educational evaluation. Christian educators are called upon to protest unfaithful and reductionistic practices and forms and to advocate more faithful alternatives where they can be discerned. The constant challenge is to name idolatries that emerge in any educational approach as it becomes a rigid paradigm.

A second consideration in the United States is what Abraham J. Heschel named in his discussion of needs (chap. 1). Needs assessment is a popular approach to educational planning and evaluation in which the careful articulation of student needs serves to guide the teaching-learning process. In a society that evidences an overwhelming preoccupation with human needs, educators must exercise discernment to distinguish the nature of those needs. A distinction must be made between persons' felt needs and their real needs. One dictum of the common cultural wisdom of the age is that student needs should be the primary determinant of educational content. A corollary of this dictum is that the educator should initiate her or his efforts by addressing felt needs, and then eventually disclose and address real needs. Following such common wisdom may result in serious inattention to the demands of God upon persons in various areas of responsibility not encompassed by the naming of needs. Heschel described this situation as the tyranny of needs with a society or culture distorting the perception of needs that are only corrected in relation to honoring divine demands upon persons.[22] This tyranny of needs is an expression of the reductionism described earlier as contextualism, activism, and personalism.

With the naming of possible conflict between Christian and cultural values, educators must also recognize points of confirmation and complementarity between the Christian faith and particular cultures. The emphasis upon critique and protest in educational evaluation may not permit appropriate affirmation. With worship and celebration at the hub of the five-task model, educators are called upon to name gratefully how God's grace has been experienced in and through the lives of others. This

22. Abraham J. Heschel, *Between God and Man: An Interpretation of Judaism from the Writings of Abraham Heschel,* ed. Fritz A. Rothschild (New York: Free Press, 1959), 129–51.

naming contributes to a sense of joy that is essential to effective Christian education.

The Five-Task Model and Evaluation

Having proposed the five-task model as an underlying form for Christian education, I must now make suggestions for evaluating each of those tasks and for maintaining a balance among them. The setting for these suggestions is the local church.

In relation to kerygma or proclamation, educators can assess the level of biblical and theological literacy among participants in the faith community and its programs. But beyond literacy is the level of commitment to God and to discipleship as a follower of Jesus Christ. Literacy and commitment levels can be addressed in educational programs and considered in the response of disciples-in-the-making. The response to kerygma is evidenced in the discernment of God's call and the living of Christian vocation by those who would follow Jesus as disciples or learners. Marianne Sawicki helpfully suggests four characteristics of Christian discipleship: a personal encounter with Jesus, a call to which one responds, a mission to testify to others about Jesus, and a following of Jesus to death.[23]

The health of any particular congregation can be evaluated in relation to their understanding and appreciation of these four characteristics of discipleship and their living out of the implications. First, do participants understand and appreciate their personal encounter and relationship with Jesus Christ? Second, do participants understand and appreciate the call of God in their lives? Third, do participants have a sense of mission as evidenced by their sharing of their faith and lives? Fourth, do participants demonstrate a commitment to follow Jesus throughout their lives even to the point of death? Not many churches keep account of the number of their martyrs, but the example of those who sacrificially serve Jesus does have an educational impact. The examples of Martin Luther King, Jr., and Mother Teresa are noteworthy, but others not gaining global recognition can be named in every congregation. Their lives

23. Marianne Sawicki, *The Gospel in History: Portrait of a Teaching Church, The Origins of Christian Education* (New York: Paulist, 1988), 60–62, 90.

give evidence to a faithful response to kerygma so that the faith is caught as well as explicitly taught.

In relation to koinonia or community, educators can assess the nature of community life and the educational efforts to initiate and sustain members of the community. These efforts include the invitation to strangers to become community members and the hospitality afforded visitors. Several questions can be considered. What is the sense of covenant and mutuality in the local church? How much time do people spend with each other outside of the formal programs? How do persons support one another in times of stress and transition? How and when are the joys and sorrows of individuals and families shared across the congregation? What binds the people together and how is a sense of connection celebrated in the life of the community? Who are involved with friendships and small group activities that sustain and support growth in Christian faith and life? The areas explored in such questions can be intentionally addressed in educational programs that both consider and foster the relational web within the faith community.

In relation to diakonia or service, educators can assess the extent to which person are trained for and engaged in active service both within and beyond the congregation. This is the outworking of Paul's admonition in Galatians 6:10: "Therefore, as we have opportunity, let us do good to all people, especially to those who belong to the family of believers." A number of questions can be raised. How are persons encouraged to acts of service and mission in educational programs, and how are they exposed to appropriate models for such outreach? How does the faith taught to believers issue in works of service not only in the church as it is gathered, but also as it is scattered? How is service as conceived and practiced by the congregation, extended beyond the bounds of the church building to include the local, regional, national, and global communities? What awareness is present in the congregation in relation to these other opportunities beyond the local congregation? How do the church's neighbors know that Christ is present in the lives of the church's members and participants? What relationships do church participants see between God's mission in the world and various local and global mission efforts of the congregation? Christian education programs can actively prepare persons for a diversity of ministries in accord with spiritual gifts and callings and provide opportunities to reflect upon their ministries in relation to the Christian faith. Education for service and mission must be an intentional component of Christian education.[24]

The task of propheteia or advocacy can also be evaluated by educators by considering the following questions. How does the local church advocate for the values of Christ's reign in the public sphere? How does a passion for Jesus issue in a passion for justice, righteousness, and peace in the life of the congregation and beyond? How do church members so express their love by making a difference in the lives of all those for whom Christ has died, including the least of his sisters and brothers? One recognizes in evangelical churches the fashionable neglect of local and national mission needs with a greater interest in international mission. David Bosch refers to this problem as "the faulty doctrine of salt water"—that traveling to foreign lands is the essence of any kind of worthy mission.[25] One also recognizes the greater interest in issues of apartheid in South Africa with a cultural blindness to the continued presence of racism in the United States. As Jesus taught, we remove the splinter from our brother's eye while we ignore the log in our own eye.

An additional question is posed for propheteia by the current ecological crisis. How do we, as local churches, care for God's creation as a heritage for future generations? We would do well to emulate the perspective of many indigenous populations who consider the heritage they are leaving to the seventh generation.

Leitourgia or worship represents the fifth task, and it too can be evaluated by educators. The primary educational emphasis to assess in relation to leitourgia is liturgical literacy, but other questions are appropriate. How are educational programs contributing to dynamic and transforming worship in the congregation? How does a sense of worship extend beyond public wor-

---

24. Two helpful resources are Arthur O. F. Bauer, *Being in Mission* (New York: Friendship, 1987); and Paul D. Gehris and Katherine A. Gehris, *The Teaching Church—Active in Mission* (Valley Forge, Penn.: Judson, 1987).

25. David J. Bosch, *Transforming Mission: Paradigm Shifts in Theology of Mission* (Maryknoll, N.Y.: Orbis, 1991), 10.

ship to affect private worship and devotion throughout the week? Educational programs can pose questions and assist persons to transfer their learning beyond the confines of Sunday mornings. Those churches that have opted for lectionary-based curricula have some built-in opportunities to link worship and educational content, but all churches can explore the connections and hold them before participants. How is the spiritual journey of persons fostered in Christian education? How is the recreative potential in various forms of worship being explored and how are opportunities for creative expression being planned in Christian education programs? People need times for sabbath and repose that can foster contemplation of the wonders of God and recover a sense of God's presence in all of life. Worship and the education for and of worship can enable us to gain God's perspective on personal and corporate life and in the process enable us to enjoy and glorify God.

The evaluative question of a balance of the five tasks requires that educators consider the educational diet of particular settings. This balance can best be understood in relation to the metaphors of a meal or of nutrition. Many evangelical and conservative churches have so stressed proclamation and community, or evangelism and body life, that little occurs in terms of service and advocacy that reach beyond the boundaries of the congregation except in very prescribed ways. Little effect is made upon developments in the community or wider society. Thus evangelical churches may be anemic or malnourished in the areas of service and advocacy, which need to be stressed to recover a sense of balance.

Churches of a more moderate or liberal stance are generally so engaged with service and advocacy that little attention may be given to gaining biblical, theological, or liturgical literacy for persons across the life span.[26] Therefore they are anemic or malnourished in the areas of proclamation and worship. Confirming such an assessment, Robert Webber suggests that litur-

26. For a discussion of issues of literacy, see Kay Kupper Berg, "Christian Literacy, the Core Curriculum, and the Urban Church," in *Urban Church Education*, ed. Donald B. Rogers (Birmingham, Ala.: Religious Education Press, 1989), 50–59.

gical renewal and liturgical evangelism are essential for mainline denominations to recover a sense of balance.[27]

A stress upon worship or liturgical renewal may also be helpful for evangelical churches if it challenges persons to see how their faith relates to wider communal and societal life. Such a stress upon worship is implied by placing leitourgia at the center of the five-task model. For evangelical churches, this implies an outworking of the Christian faith in terms of service and advocacy. In other words, faith must find expression in terms of works. This is the message of the Book of James. Liberal and mainline churches may stress works to the exclusion of understanding and appreciating the Christian faith that is a relative strength in evangelical churches.

Historical breaches have existed between liberal and evangelical segments of the church. What is suggested in this analysis is the healing of these historical breaches that have plagued the Christian church to restore balance on the global scale. But on the local level this requires willingness to learn from other theological traditions in fulfilling the multifaceted educational ministry suggested by the five-task model. A comprehensive and holistic response to the gospel demands faithfulness in all the tasks.

But beyond this broader agenda, the question of balance must consider the historical heritage of a particular church and the exposure that any group of learners has had to the central tasks given to the Christian church in fulfilling the mission of God. One must also recognize the unique calling of particular congregations, given their discernment of local challenges. But in general, the five-task model suggests that each of the five tasks requires attention if Christians are to be faithful in their educational ministries over time and declare the whole will or counsel of God (Acts 20:27). If not, a full meal will not be served and God's people will not be adequately nourished.

Conclusion: The Risks of Teaching/Learning

With all that has been said so far, Christian educators may conclude that educational evaluation is a complex and over-

27. Robert Webber, *Celebrating Our Faith: Evangelism Through Worship* (San Francisco: Harper and Row, 1986).

whelming responsibility. Complex, yes, but not overwhelming: We are in partnership with the triune God in our efforts. Such a partnership calls for the best possible efforts while being aware of human limitations and the risks of teaching and learning. Both teachers and students are called upon to be vulnerable, to be open to the possibility of conversion and transformation. Conversion denotes a turning with real costs for the students as well as the teachers.

Teaching is risky business, and no absolute guarantees can be provided that any teaching, even if it is carefully planned, practiced, and evaluated, will result in learning (see chap. 5). It was noted that the active cooperation of participants, of students, is indispensable for teaching to result in learning. Thus teaching can be shared, but not imposed upon students. This is suggested by Paulo Freire's description of banking education (chap. 5). The challenge is for teachers and students to work cooperatively in the process of education.

In addition, the Christian teacher does have the promise of the resurrected Lord Jesus Christ in exploring the nature of divine and human cooperation in education. Christian teachers have the promise of an authority and a presence in teaching that can make the essential difference through the ministry of the Holy Spirit:

"All authority in heaven and earth has been given to me. Therefore go and make disciples of all nations, baptizing them in the name of the Father and of the Son and of the Holy Spirit, and teaching them to obey everything I have commanded you. And surely I will be with you always, to the very end of the age." [Matt. 28:18–20]

Risks are always present, but they are well worth taking in the teaching and learning of which Jesus invites us to partake at his table.

The prayer that accompanies this work is for the renewal of Christian education as Christians seriously and joyfully respond to God's call to be faithful in their thought and practice.

Select Bibliography

Historical Principles

Boys, Mary C. *Educating in Faith: Maps and Visions.* San Francisco: Harper and Row, 1989.

Burgess, Harold W. *An Invitation to Religious Education.* Birmingham, Ala.: Religious Education Press, 1975.

Fackre, Dorothy, and Gabriel Fackre. *Christian Basics: A Primer for Pilgrims.* Grand Rapids: Eerdmans, 1991.

Gaebelein, Frank E. *The Pattern of God's Truth: Problems of Integration in Christian Education.* New York: Oxford University Press, 1954.

Gangel, Kenneth O., and Warren S. Benson. *Christian Education: Its History and Philosophy.* Chicago: Moody, 1983.

LeBar, Lois E. *Education That Is Christian.* Old Tappan, N.J.: Revell, 1981.

Osmer, Richard R. *A Teachable Spirit: Recovering the Teaching Office in the Church.* Louisville: Westminster/John Knox, 1990.

Pazmiño, Robert W. *Foundational Issues in Christian Education: An Introduction in Evangelical Perspective.* Grand Rapids: Baker, 1988.

Richards, Lawrence O. *A Theology of Christian Education.* Grand Rapids: Zondervan, 1975.

Sawicki, Marianne. *The Gospel in History: Portrait of a Teaching Church, The Origins of Christian Education.* New York: Paulist, 1988.

Stackhouse, Max L. *Public Theology and Political Economy.* Grand Rapids: Eerdmans, 1980.

Contemporary Principles

Costas, Orlando E. *Liberating News: A Theology of Contextual Evangelization.* Grand Rapids: Eerdmans, 1989.

Gaventa, Beverly Roberts. *From Darkness to Light: Aspects of Conversion in the New Testament.* Philadelphia: Fortress, 1986.

Gillespie, V. Bailey. *The Dynamics of Religious Conversion: Identity and Transformation.* Birmingham, Ala.: Religious Education Press, 1991.

Johnson, Susanne. *Christian Spiritual Formation in the Church and Classroom.* Nashville: Abingdon, 1989.

Nelson, C. Ellis. *How Faith Matures.* Louisville: Westminster/John Knox, 1989.

Peace, Richard. "The Conversion of the Twelve: A Study of the Process of Conversion in the New Testament." Ph.D. dissertation, University of Natal, South Africa, 1990.

Seymour, Jack L., and Donald E. Miller, eds. *Contemporary Approaches to Christian Education.* Nashville: Abingdon, 1982.

————. *Theological Approaches to Christian Education.* Nashville: Abingdon, 1990.

Shelp, Earl E., and Ronald H. Sunderland. *The Pastor as Teacher.* New York: Pilgrim, 1989.

Wilhoit, Jim. *Christian Education and the Search for Meaning.* 2d ed. Grand Rapids: Baker, 1991.

Williamson, Clark M., and Ronald J. Allen. *The Teaching Minister.* Louisville: Westminster/John Knox, 1991.

Educational Structures

Bailyn, Bernard. *Education in the Forming of American Society: Needs and Opportunities for Study.* New York: Norton, 1960.

Cremin, Lawrence A. *Popular Education and Its Discontents.* San Francisco: Harper and Row, 1990.

————. *Traditions of American Education.* New York: Basic, 1977.

Cully, Iris V., and Kendig B. Cully, eds. *Harper's Encyclopedia of Religious Education*. San Francisco: Harper and Row, 1990.

La Belle, Thomas J. *Nonformal Education in Latin America and the Caribbean: Stability, Reform and Revolution*. New York: Praeger, 1986.

Miller, Donald E. *Story and Context: An Introduction to Christian Education*. Nashville: Abingdon, 1987.

Moore, Allen J. *Religious Education as Social Transformation*. Birmingham, Ala.: Religious Education Press, 1989.

Postman, Neil, and Charles Weingartner. *Teaching as Subversive Activity*. New York: Delacorte, 1969.

White, James W. *Intergenerational Religious Education*. Birmingham, Ala.: Religious Education Press, 1988.

Educational Content

Eisner, Elliot W. *The Educational Imagination: On the Design and Evaluation of School Programs*. 2d ed. New York: Macmillan, 1985.

Griggs, Donald L. *Teaching Teachers to Teach: A Basic Manual for Church Teachers*. Nashville: Abingdon, 1974.

Groome, Thomas H. *Christian Religious Education: Sharing Our Story and Vision*. San Francisco: Harper and Row, 1980.

———. *Sharing Faith: A Comprehensive Approach to Religious Education and Pastoral Ministry*. San Francisco: Harper and Row, 1991.

Harris, Maria. *Fashion Me a People: Curriculum in the Church*. Louisville: Westminster/John Knox, 1989.

———. *Teaching and Religious Imagination: An Essay in the Theology of Teaching*. San Francisco: Harper and Row, 1987.

Lee, James Michael. *The Content of Religious Instruction: A Social Science Approach*. Birmingham, Ala.: Religious Education Press, 1985.

Richards, Lawrence O. *Creative Bible Teaching*. Chicago: Moody, 1970.

Schipani, Daniel S. *Religious Education Encounters Liberation Theology*. Birmingham, Ala.: Religious Education Press, 1988.

Wilson, Douglas. *Recovering the Lost Tools of Learning: An Approach to Distinctly Christian Education*. Wheaton: Crossway, 1991.

Wolterstorff, Nicholas P. *Educating for Responsible Action.* Grand Rapids: Eerdmans, 1980.

Wyckoff, D. Campbell. *Theory and Design of Christian Education Curriculum.* Philadelphia: Westminster, 1961.

Educational Methods

Bruce, A. B. *The Training of the Twelve.* Reprint. Grand Rapids: Kregel, 1971.

Freire, Paulo. *Pedagogy of the Oppressed.* Translated by Myra Bergman Ramos. New York: Seabury, 1970.

Grassi, Joseph A. *Teaching the Way: Jesus, the Early Church and Today.* Lanham, Md.: University Press of America, 1982.

Hill, Brian. *Faith at the Blackboard: Issues Facing the Christian Teacher.* Grand Rapids: Eerdmans, 1982.

Horne, Herman H. *The Teaching Techniques of Jesus: How Jesus Taught.* 1920. Reprint. Grand Rapids: Kregel, 1971.

Lee, James Michael. *The Flow of Religious Instruction.* Birmingham, Ala.: Religious Education Press, 1973.

LeFever, Marlene D. *Creative Teaching Methods.* Elgin, Ill.: David C. Cook, 1985.

Palmer, Parker J. *To Know as We Are Known: A Spirituality of Education.* San Francisco: Harper and Row, 1983.

Stein, Robert. *The Method and Message of Jesus' Teaching.* Philadelphia: Westminster, 1978.

Wyckoff, D. Campbell. *The Tasks of Christian Education.* Philadelphia: Westminster, 1955.

Educational Evaluation

Bellack, Arno A., and Herbert M. Kliebard. *Curriculum and Evaluation.* Berkeley: McCutchan, 1977.

Eggleston, John. *The Sociology of the School Curriculum.* London: Routledge and Kegan Paul, 1977.

Eisner, Elliot. *The Educational Imagination: On the Design and Evaluation of School Programs.* 2d. ed. New York: Macmillan, 1985.

Green, Thomas F. *The Activities of Teaching.* New York: McGraw-Hill, 1971.

Heschel, Abraham J.. *Between God and Man: An Interpretation of Judaism from the Writings of Abraham Heschel.* Edited by Fritz A. Rothschild. New York: Free Press, 1959.

Nelson, C. Ellis. *Using Evaluation in Theological Education.* Nashville: Discipleship Resources, 1975.

Spaulding, Helen F., ed. *Evaluation and Christian Education: Discussion of Some Theological, Educational and Practical Issues.* New York: National Council of Churches in the U.S.A., Office of Publication and Duplication, 1960.

Wyckoff, D. Campbell. *How to Evaluate Your Christian Education Program.* Philadelphia: Westminster, 1962.

Index